HOW TO BLOG:

Start A Blog for Profit. Make Money Blogging with many Strategies and Start a Profitable Blog to Build a Passive Income Business

MARK GROWT

© **Copyright 2019 by Mark Growt - All rights reserved.**

The content contained within this book may not be reproduced, duplicated or transmitted without direct written permission from the author or the publisher.

Under no circumstances will any blame or legal responsibility be held against the publisher, or author, for any damages, reparation, or monetary loss due to the information contained within this book. Either directly or indirectly.

Legal Notice:

This book is copyright protected. This book is only for personal use. You cannot amend, distribute, sell, use, quote or paraphrase any part, or the content within this book, without the consent of the author or publisher.

Disclaimer Notice:

Please note the information contained within this document is for educational and entertainment purposes only. All effort has been executed to present accurate, up to date, and reliable, complete information. No warranties of any kind are declared or implied. Readers acknowledge that the author is not engaging in the rendering of legal, financial, medical or professional advice. The content within this book has been derived from various sources. Please consult a licensed professional before attempting any techniques outlined in this book.

By reading this document, the reader agrees that under no circumstances is the author responsible for any losses, direct or indirect, which are incurred as a result of the use of information contained within this document, including, but not limited to, — errors, omissions, or inaccuracies.

Table of contents

INTRODUCTION 6

CHAPTER 1 GETTING STARTED 9
    DECIDE ON YOUR CONTENT BUCKETS 9
    COME UP WITH YOUR BLOG'S NAME 12
    CHOOSE A BLOGGING PLATFORM 16
    PURCHASE A DOMAIN FOR YOUR BLOG 17
    CREATE AN EMAIL ACCOUNT 19
    CREATE A CONTENT CALENDAR 19

CHAPTER 2 POSITION YOUR BLOG AS A VOICE OF AUTHORITY 22

CHAPTER 3 OUTSOURCE TO BUILD A BLOGGING TEAM . 30
    OUTSOURCE SLOWLY 32

CHAPTER 4 CREATING A LEAD MAGNET 35

CHAPTER 5 THE DASHBOARD 44

CHAPTER 6 CUSTOMIZING YOUR WEBSITE'S APPEARANCE 53

CHAPTER 7 BLOG MONETIZATION – DIGITAL PRODUCTS (EBOOKS) 60
    EMAIL MARKETING TO SELL MORE 64
    LET'S GET PRACTICAL 66

CHAPTER 8 MONETIZING THROUGH SPONSORED POSTS 69
    WHAT IS THE EARNING POTENTIAL WITH SPONSORED CONTENT? 70
    WHY SPONSORED POSTS ARE AN AWESOME REVENUE GENERATING TOOL 70

How to Secure Sponsored Posts on Your Blog 71
The Types of Sponsored Post Options to Work With 72

CHAPTER 9 WEBSITE FLIPPING 74

CHAPTER 10 LISTICLE BLOGGING 80
How is Money Made? 80
Creating Your Listicle 81

CHAPTER 11 HOW TO BUILD AN EMAIL LIST 84
Gathering email 85
Presentation page 86
Making email 86

CHAPTER 12 TYPES OF BLOGS 89
The Personal Blog 89
The Personal Brand Blog 90
The Corporate Blog 91
The Niche Blog 92
Case Study or Test Blogs 93
Guest Blogging 94
Specialty Explicit 95
Discovering sites to post on 95
Composing the post 96
Discover what is working 97

CHAPTER 13 TYPES OF CONTENT THAT CAN SKY-ROCKET YOUR BLOG TRAFFIC 98

CHAPTER 14 BEST BLOGGING RESOURCES 110
Hosting Providers 110
Plugins and Tools 111
Affiliate Networks 113

SELF-PUBLISHING RESOURCES 114
PRODUCT TOOLS 114
MEMBERSHIP SITES 115

CHAPTER 15 HOW TO USE ALL THESE METHODS 116

CHAPTER 16 COMMON MISTAKES 120

CONCLUSION 125

Introduction

Blogging today has become a profitable business. One can make easy and big money by Blogging. All you need is a passion and interest to earn that money. The blogosphere is nothing but a web of connections made by links from blog to blog. When people browse, they are always searching for articles of interest and sometimes come across articles they never thought they would even go through. The reader sometimes suddenly find these articles so interesting that they read the whole article. When do you think this arousing of keen interest happens to the reader? This would only happen, if the writer has put their heart and soul to write the article with all the passion and research to produce this effective article. This is what, all writing a Blog is all about. Let us check in this article, how you can become a successful Blogger in a few easy steps.

To start with the first step, I would say that the introductory part of the article is very important. Whenever you begin to write the introduction, it has to be interesting because only an interesting and catchy introduction will make the reader read more. You need to make your introduction more professional and interesting to catch the imagination of the reader. Have a great introduction, so that readers can decide to link to your article, or even submit it to a social book-marking site. Speaking of paragraphs, try and make relevant paragraphs, so that there is a link in all the paragraphs. Be precise, clear and interesting in what you write. Don't break important information in the paragraphs because a person may tend to lose the link and, in the bargain, lose interest as well.

Make your article attractive to be successful. Just writing only a simple article will make the article dull and boring. Make it interesting by adding visual elements to it. Describe your writing with visual content, so that it looks attractive and makes it simpler and easier for the reader to grasp. Sometimes your sentence may not make much sense to the reader, but the picture content will give a clear idea of what you would like to represent and convey to the reader. You can be creative and put your imagination in pictures and force the reader to imagine in the same way. This is one way you can become a successful Blogger.

Create a structure for your article. What I mean is organize your content in a manner that is easy to understand. When you want to emphasize on a certain point create a heading and make it bold. Try and explain in detail with simple and easy language. Highlighting key pieces of your article through the use of bold type or emphasizing words through italics, lets your readers know where to focus and it is handy for those who are skimming. Make your article easy to read by choosing the right font size. Line spacing is also important, so take care. Add links and block quotes where required. Be professional, impressive and creative to make yourself a successful Blogger.

This guide will take you through how to set up your blog and make money from it. Read on!!!

Chapter 1 Getting Started

When starting a lifestyle blog, there are a few basic elements you need to check off your list.

Completing these steps will ensure that you're ready to start crafting content on a regular basis and set you up for future success.

Perhaps you already have a blog and you want to take it to the next level. Or maybe you've been tossing around the idea of starting a blog for quite some time but you just don't know where to start. I want to help you with that.

Here's what you'll need to do:

Decide on Your Content Buckets

The first question you should ask yourself is "what do you want to blog about?" Lifestyle bloggers have hundreds of options of things to write about. Determine what your blog will be about before you get into more detailed and complex areas of blogging. It's important that you get the basics out of the way first.

There are hundreds of other things you could blog about that would still fall under the *lifestyle* umbrella.

There are many different bucket options you can create content in if you want to be a lifestyle blogger. Whether you want to write about fashion, beauty, food, healthy living, home and garden, travel, city life, crafts, or something different, you'll need to determine what your content categories are based on your desire to blog about them. Some bloggers choose to only write about fashion, while other bloggers create content around food, travel, and city life.

Some bloggers choose to only post content about one particular subject. For instance: food and/or recipes. Their content buckets may be categorized by certain types of recipes, like vegan recipes, vegetarian recipes, beef recipes, pork recipes, etc. Or categorized by breakfast recipes, lunch recipes, dinner recipes, and cocktail recipes. You get the picture.

It's also a good idea to think about your target audience. Would they be mostly male or female? Older or younger? Consider their interests, hobbies, and passions when you start to hone in on what your blog will be about.

There is no limit on how many categories you choose to have on your blog, but it is important to have a good understanding of how each of these will serve your blog overall. For the sake of consistency, you'll want to make sure there is an even mix of posts in each category on your blog.

Remember that when you start a lifestyle blog, you're becoming one of thousands of people who already have a blog much like your own. It's easy for certain lifestyle categories to be a bit oversaturated, so put as much of your own uniqueness and personality into your content as you can so that it stands out from the rest. It's okay to be different.

Once you have your blog buckets decided, it will be helpful to your readers to have them categorized by individual pages on your blog. This means that you can have them as tabs in your sub-header, links in your sidebar, or really however you want them laid out on your site. The benefit in this is having readers click the tab/link when they want to go directly to a page of posts listed under *only* that category. Say you're creating a DIY-themed blog and one of your visitors wants to see only posts about DIY decor. They'd benefit greatly from being able to click a tab or subtab specifically about DIY decor. This would mean they no longer have to scroll through every post and every page just to find what they're looking for.

Come up with Your Blog's Name

Since I didn't take it very seriously from the get-go and had assumed nobody would read my blog anyway, I used a name that didn't fit the style of the blog I was trying to create. By the time I started blog #2 and #3, I had learned the importance of having a solid blog name.

Remember, you have to live with it. If you plan on keeping your blog around for awhile, it should absolutely have a name that you feel proud of and feel comfortable saying out loud when people ask you about it. (It also helps to imagine that name on your business card.)

If you're not sure where to even start with coming up with a name for your blog, don't stress. A lot of bloggers struggle with this first step because they know it sets the tone for their entire website and they end up putting a lot of pressure on themselves. I did the same thing for every blog that I started.

Here are a few simple tips for coming up with a blog name that you won't hate:

Identify the Topics You Want to Cover in Your Blog

Having a clear understanding of the topics you'd like to blog about will help you figure out a name for your blog. What would you like your blog to be about? Are you planning to post about beauty and makeup? Maybe you want to blog about wine. Are you an aspiring foodie blogger? Do you want to show off your own personal style? Whatever your topic may be, having it clearly defined will help you kick-off your blog name brainstorm.

Start a Word Brainstorm

Now that you have decided on the topics you would like to cover in your blog, you can start brainstorming words to use in your blog's name. Whatever the case may be, you should start by writing down words associated with your topic. If you are struggling to come up with creative words that relate to your blog's topic, bust out the thesaurus and ask for some help. Let's use the "wine" topic as an example. If you consider yourself a wino, then you probably already know some wine terms and lingo that could be appropriate to include in your blog's name. For instance, you may start to jot down words like bottle, glass, cellar, cork, vine, grape, vineyard, reserve, etc.

Then, add in extra words that will help define your blog's theme. If you want to blog about wine in a certain region, you could add words about the location of the wine you want to blog about.

Once you have a list of words that relate to your topic, you can start to circle the words you love and cross out the words you are certain you don't want to use.

Determine Your Blog's Tone

When future visitors come to your site, they'll quickly get a taste of what your tone is by the way you write your blog posts, the style and theme of your website, and the images you post. It's important to set the tone for your blog before you get started and it will also help you find the right name for your blog. Whether your tone includes humor and jokes or is serious and factual, determining the tone of your blog and your voice will help you hone in on the perfect name.

For example: with my blog, *Breezy and Brazen*, I knew that I found a name I liked when I found two words that had great alliteration and both were adjectives that described my personality.

Combine Your Tone with Your Word Brainstorm

Now that you have a shorter list of words from your brainstorm and have determined the tone of your blog, you can start to put catchy phrases together that may work as potential blog names. If you want to be clever and creative with some wine terminology, you can jot down things like: Off the Vine, Laura Uncorked, Vicky's Vineyard, Sass in a Glass, etc. As you come up with different titles, you will start to pay special attention to those that stand out as being a great blog name.

Once you've selected the phrase or title you love most, make the final decision on whether or not this is the blog name you want to keep forever. If it is, do a quick search on the Internet and make sure it hasn't already been taken by someone else. If it has, go back to your top selected phrases and find something else you love.

When your blog officially has a name you love, write it down in big, bold words and let it sink in.

Don't be too quick to purchase a domain with a name you haven't spent some time thinking about it. Remember, you're investing in yourself and in your blog. If you want it to last, you'll want to select a name that you'll love for more than just a day, month, or even a year. Make sure it's something you want to keep and something that signifies yourself as a brand.

Choose a Blogging Platform

After you have chosen the perfect name for your blog, it is time to select a blogging platform. This is where your blog will be hosted. If you already have a basic understanding of blogging, you may have an idea of what your best options are for selecting a platform. If you have never blogged before, now would be the time to start researching which platform will be right for you.

There isn't a right or wrong answer when it comes to selecting the program you want to use to create your content, but some people prefer different features over others. If you want something simple and easy to use, you might want to try Google Blogger, otherwise known as blogspot.com. (Beware, though, if you plan on advancing your skills as a blogger, you may want to consider something a bit more intermediate or advanced. I'll explain that at the end of this chapter.) If you have some intermediate to advanced HTML skills or want access to additional features and plugins with your blog, it might be a good idea to use WordPress. There are many benefits to choosing a platform that has an array of plugins that can help your blog grow and succeed.

Personally, I prefer using WordPress now that I have a couple years of blogging under my belt. That's mainly due in part to the fact that it offers so many plugins that help me stay on track and organized. I also love the on-page optimization abilities that are offered by WordPress. I'll get into those helpful plugins and capabilities a bit later in

Purchase a Domain for Your Blog

Once you have a web host for your blog, it'll be time to move forward with owning your own little corner on the Internet. To own your space, you will need to purchase your web domain. The name of your blog will most likely be the domain name you choose, unless it's already been purchased by someone else.

For example: if you selected the name *Off the Vine* for your blog, but the domain "offthevine.com" has already been taken, you can try things like "offthevineblog.com," "offthevine-blog.com," or "off-the-vine.com." Don't be immediately discouraged if you can't purchase the domain you originally wanted.

There are multiple reasons why registering your domain name is a good idea. Take the following reasons into account if you are on the fence about purchasing your web domain.

- If you ever decided to change your web host, your domain name goes with you. This means that any regular visitors you have coming to your blog who knew your site name as "www.yourblogname.blogspot.com" or "www.yourblogname.wordpress.com" would not have to be informed about you changing your site to "www.yourblogname.com."

- <u>Owning your domain name also gives you credibility and helps with SEO rankings.</u>

- <u>Domain names are memorable, making it easier for you to communicate to others what your web URL is. They also look more professional on business cards.</u>

- <u>Domain names are typically inexpensive. Most are under $20, with a renewal fee that is almost always less than $15/year.</u>

There are numerous sites you can use to purchase your web domain. I recommend browsing online to find the best plan for you.

Create an Email Account

In order to not lose important blog-related emails in your personal inbox, you'll want to have a space dedicated to your blog only. If anyone wants to reach out to you to discuss collaboration opportunities or brand features, it will help to have a blog email address.

One of the benefits of purchasing a domain for your blog is that you'll have the ability to create an email account using your domain. For instance: susan@blogname.com. It appears more professional and keeps everything neat and organized.

Create a Content Calendar

Now that you have your blog created and you own your domain, it's time to create a basic content calendar so that you can stay on track with your publishing. You may even want to have a few blog posts ready to go before your website actually goes live so that you have some various content on your blog from day one.

Your content calendar can be online or in a planner if you prefer to write things down on paper. I personally prefer to use Google Calendar in case I need to sync any of my events with another user's calendar.

It's important for you to choose your blogging frequency. Some bloggers choose to post more than four times per week, while others only post a few times per month. If posting every other day is too rigorous for your schedule then set a frequency that allows you to be more flexible.

Your ideal blogging routine might be as simple as one post per week. You may also find that your blogging frequency is dependant on how often you're feeling inspired to create a new post.

There isn't a "one size fits all" approach to creating a blogging schedule. What is important is that you find a routine that you can stick to over the long term and doesn't make you feel overwhelmed after just a few weeks of going at it. When you're experimenting with your blogging routine, you may also want to consider your different content categories and how often you want to post about each one.

If you co-write a blog with others, a content calendar will be even more beneficial because you can provide full transparency over who is in charge of what posts right on your calendar. This will help all writers of your blog stay on track and have a full understanding of who is working on what articles.

How I Failed at Blogging Basics

When I first started out, I didn't do any research on which platform would be best for first-time blogging. Instead, I went with the only option I knew at the time, Google Blogger. It was super simple to use and offered the basics of what I needed for writing and sharing content, but it came with no additional tools to enhance SEO value, plugins that worked *for* my blog, or ways to customize my site.

I also *still* often struggle with maintaining a content calendar for my blog. I really tend to drop the ball when I'm traveling because I plan to work around my vacations but then have a hard time catching up when I get back. I've failed time and time again with sticking to my original post publishing dates and it always winds up making me feel overwhelmed.

Too many planned posts can turn into no posts at all. It's easy to look at a calendar and say "I want to publish a new post every single day this month," but the likeliness of that actually happening (especially if you have a full-time job, enjoy having a social life, and require at least 8 hours of sleep per night) is pretty slim. I learned the hard way when I saw all of my tasks turn red and I didn't get the chance to cross them off because I excessively overplanned and underestimated how difficult it would be to keep up with creating content.

Chapter 2 Position Your Blog As A Voice Of Authority

If you set up a restaurant, what would you like it to be known for? A relaxed place with cheap food for students? A homey restaurant for families? Or would you like to offer candlelight dinners for romantic 50-plussers?

If you try to target everyone with your restaurant, then you end up appealing to no one. Rowdy students may irritate romantic couples. Posh diners pull up their noses at hungry bicyclists sitting down in their Lycra. You can't cater to everyone with your restaurant, and it's the same for your blog.

Just like your restaurant targets a specific audience (students or 50+ couples) with a specific product (cheap food or candlelit dinners), your blog should target a specific audience with a specific topic.

You may want to share budgeting tips (*topic*) to help students (*audience*) with their finances, or you may want to help 50-plussers (*audience*) plan for their retirement (*topic*). You can't appeal to both students and 50-plussers with the same blog, because they face different challenges, have different levels of knowledge about finance, and they use different words to talk about financial issues.

The *what* you offer is your blog purpose. It summarizes in one sentence how you help your readers.

In this chapter you learn:

- Why you need a blog purpose
- What is a good blog purpose
- How to define your own blog purpose
- The 5 mistakes you must avoid when defining your blog purpose

Why you need a blog purpose

Your blog purpose is your mission—but I don't like to use that word, as it reminds me of corporate mission statements like: *We are committed to combining cutting-edge solutions with excellent customer service.* *Bleergh* That's not the gobbledygook you're looking for. Let's have a look at what you do need...

What is a good blog purpose?

A good blog purpose attracts, energizes, and motivates people. When you have a clear purpose, readers feel you genuinely care about them.

Your purpose should be concrete and specific, because fluffy or vague statements don't galvanize your readers.

You don't require a grand statement. You don't need to change the whole world. You can start small. You just need a purpose you feel passionate about. A few examples:

- Help students manage their finances so they can graduate with lower debts
- Help 1,000 single mothers start their own online business
- Get rid of gobbledygook on small business websites

Let's say you're a personal trainer, and you're starting a blog to promote your fitness center. What could your blog purpose be?

You might want to promote your center and talk about your events, but initially nobody is interested in that. When you just promote your business, readers quickly get enough of your blog.

Your blog becomes more appealing to your ideal reader if you share tips on, for instance, staying healthy. Your purpose could be to inspire more middle-aged men to get active—you can share simple tips to relieve stress or explain exercises to remain trim.

A good blog purpose inspires your target audience. The more specific you can make it, the better. *Sharing finance tips* is rather generic. *Helping students manage their finances so they graduate with lower debt* is more specific and more inspirational.

How to define your own blog purpose

You need to be passionate about your blog purpose. But your ideal reader also needs to be energized by your blog purpose. In short, you need to find a purpose at the crossroads of what your ideal reader wants to read and what you want to write about.

What keeps him up at night? What is he afraid of losing?

Now, write down a list of topics that you could help your ideal reader with. Don't worry too much about whether you have the knowledge or not, just write down the topics that you feel are beneficial to your ideal reader.

Once you have a list of 7 or 8 topics, select your favorite and turn it into your blog purpose by finishing a sentence that starts with *I want to ...*

You can write a positive or a negative purpose. For instance:

Positive:

I want to help small business owners write web copy that sells

Negative:

I want to eradicate gobbledygook and boring statements from small business websites

Try to make your purpose as specific as possible, and remain focused on your ideal reader. Don't feel you need to get the perfect purpose today.

Purposes evolve and get better over time—just like a Rioja Gran Reserva is richer and has more body than a fruity Rioja wine. Give yourself time.

> The 5 mistakes you must avoid when defining your blog purpose

Mistake 1

One of the biggest mistakes you can make is choosing a purpose you don't feel passionate about. If you're not passionate, you'll struggle to keep up a regular posting schedule. Moreover, when your writing lacks passion, your blog quickly becomes bland and monotonous.

A spark of enthusiasm will always shine through and make your writing livelier and more fascinating. So choose a topic you love and care about.

Mistake 2

You might be worried that you're not an authority on the topic your readers are interested in. But you don't need to be an expert when you start your blog—as long as you're committed to learning more. I had a huge amount to learn about copywriting and blogging when I started Enchanting Marketing, and I still enjoy learning more each week.

You can always find people who are more expert than you, but that's not the point. There are also people who know less than you do. So just get started. Write for beginners first, and grow your expertise while writing your blog. Your audience can evolve while your knowledge grows.

Mistake 3

You may be concerned that too many other bloggers have a similar purpose as you. This is something you definitely shouldn't worry about.

I started a blog about writing and blogging in November 2012. At that time there were hundreds of blogs about these topics, and some of them—like Copyblogger—were already hugely popular. I saw this as an advantage, as I could write guest posts for Copyblogger and piggyback off their audience.

Facing "competition" from many blogs is a good sign, because it proves that people are interested in your topic.

If your purpose is totally unique, you should be worried, because there might not be anybody interested in what you have to say. For instance, I like to watch long track speed skating, but how many people would want to read a weekly post about long track speed skating?

Mistake 4

You may be tempted to write about what you like, not what your readers want to read. This is often a problem for more mature blogs. After you've written about the same topic for a year or more, you feel the temptation to widen your scope. Widening your scope is fine, but don't extend into areas that leave your readers cold.

Let's look at an example. Imagine you're selling a social media app. Your ideal reader is a small business owner called Charles who is seriously active on social media. As a software developer, you have a lot of knowledge about product development, start-up management, and software.

Charles is not interested in hearing about start-up management and product development—even if you are passionate about it. He'd like you to teach him how to network and win clients using social media. And if you've written enough about social media, you might want to start writing about email marketing, blogging, or other marketing activities. Because that's how you can help Charles grow his business. Your purpose could evolve from *I want to help small businesses to network using social media* to *I want to help small businesses win business with online marketing*.

Mistake 5

Don't get stuck trying to define your perfect purpose. You can spend hours, days, or even months considering your purpose and dismissing each suggestion as soon as you write it down.

Define a temporary purpose now, work through the remainder of this book, and then re-visit your purpose again.

Consider your purpose a work in progress and move on. Your blog can evolve over time.

Chapter 3 Outsource To Build A Blogging Team

"A successful team is a group of many hands but of one mind." — Bill Bethel

We obviously run a bigger operation than you if you're just starting out, but that doesn't mean you can't build a team from Day 1. Blogging is not and never has been a solo job, regardless what some "blogging gurus" say. You need mentors, teachers, and advisors above you to learn from—these are your virtual board of directors. You need readers to read, followers to follow, and clients and customers to buy (when you have something to sell). You need friends, colleagues, JV (joint venture) partners, and family to support you on your journey.

Sure you can learn it all and do it all yourself, but why would you? Everyone shares the same 24 hours in one day. Do it all, and you'll burn yourself out or live and work a lonely life. Working from home can lead to seclusion, even if you're writing for the masses. Building a team is for your overall health and well-being as a person and profession.

Admittedly, there is a lot of debate about the issue of outsourcing: Will your blog still be viewed as authentic and genuine if you start delegating duties related to it? Will you slowly lose touch with your readers because you are no longer involved in some aspects of running your blog?

We view outsourcing this way: **Our primary task as bloggers is to create and produce compelling and useful content for our readers.** That is the one job we will not outsource. Every other activity concerning the blog is secondary to creating and producing content. Therefore, outsourcing other activities will not take away from the authenticity of our blogs, but will enable us to focus more on the primary task of making great content.

After all, we worked so hard crafting and developing our unique voice, there's no way to outsource that. There are ways to shortcut our efforts, but publishing an unauthentic written piece that has our names on it is not one of them.

With the end goal of producing great content, we have no problems outsourcing our blogs' technical administration and graphic design, ebook editing and design, photography work, and basic web research work. Of course, you may have to do all these things yourself when you first blog, but once you gain traction and there is some revenue coming in, outsourcing is viable.

Outsourcing Tip: *Schedule time to research possible outsourcers.* Get recommendations from colleagues and friends for possible outsourcers. Read testimonials and reviews, view portfolios, and interview via email, on the phone, or in-person. Put effort in the beginning for a better chance of securing quality outsourcers from the start. Remember, it takes less time to train a good person, than fire, search, hire, and train another person, only

to start all over again if yet another doesn't meet your expectations.

Outsource Slowly

Determining the ideal time to start outsourcing is different for every blogger, but a typical sign is when you notice your work-life begins to suffer from the imbalance. At this point, you'll decide an additional pair of hands is what you need to keep the blog running.

WARNING: Outsourcing is not easy at first. It takes a lot of time and patience. But when you find the ideal outsourcer(s), we assure you that the rewards are great!

Now that the warning is out of the way, it's best to start slowly when you're ready to outsource. Delegate duties one at a time to one outsourcer at a time, especially if you've never had the experience of hiring someone before. A quality outsource relationship depends on your ability to communicate your needs and desires effectively and efficiently.

Remember KISS: Keep It Simple, Stupid! You may know what you want, but unless you explicitly write it out or tell her, she will not know what to expect and will perform based on your instructions. Only when you are completely satisfied with the way a particular duty or person works out, then you can delegate something else.

The most important thing is to remember *you* are supervising this, and *you* are still responsible for the end result. Your name is attached to the blog. Delegation means having the luxury of others to help you with certain duties, with you in control of the direction and goals of the work. You don't want to redo work you're unsatisfied with, spending more time than you would have if you had done it yourself in the first place.

Areas to consider outsourcing are: sponsorship deals, email responses, social media interaction, technical issues, etc. There are bloggers who believe they ought to handle these things themselves, because it keeps them closer to the readers. It all depends on you—it's important to do whatever feels right and keeps you producing the content you want for your readers.

However, a productive entrepreneur, which you strive to be as a professional blogger, knows her value. For example, if your sponsor pays you $300 a blog post, and you can produce a high-quality blog post in one hour (which means writing the post, finding and editing a Pinterest-pinnable image, making sure all the appropriate SEO is applied to the post, publishing, then sharing it on a social media sites, etc.). Then, you make $300 per hour—which is a great place to be! However, if you know you can write the blog post in fifteen minutes and delegate the other work to someone for $10 and an hour to do even more social media promotion and publicity (which will give the post even more visibility), then you made $290 in approximately twenty minutes (five minutes to delegate the work via email). That's $300/hour versus $870/hour ($290 * three 20-minute periods)—a huge difference in value and worth as a professional blogger.

Outsourcing Tip: *Always put your brand first.* When you're ready to allow guest bloggers to post on your blog, you have the final say in the content published. You should always exert your right to deny any guest post because of tone, style, and especially for topic.

Chapter 4 Creating A Lead Magnet

As much as you want people to join your email list, they typically won't do it just to be nice. Like anything else in life, people will take action when they feel there is something in it for them.

One of the best ways to get people to join your e-mail list is to offer what's referred to as a lead magnet. A lead magnet is a free gift or piece of information you offer someone in exchange for trusting you enough to join your e-mail list.

This is often times a short informational product in the form of a pdf or audio file that adds value to your target audience.

The best way to think of something to turn into a lead magnet is to make a list of questions and problems that your ideal reader might run into. Then, research and write a short guide to solving those problems.

For example: If you have a blog about Online Dating, write a short guide about the secrets to writing an attractive profile. Then offer guide as a free gift to anyone that joins your newsletter. Dangling that carrot in front of people works really well since they get something of value in exchange.

The key to this working is you choosing to make something to give away that adds massive value to your targeted audience. Don't fall into the trap of thinking that you shouldn't make this free gift too good. Many people think that since they will be giving it away for free it's ok to make it of questionable quality. That is not the case.

If someone does sign up for your newsletter in exchange for your lead magnet, the content of that lead magnet will be his or her first impression of you. Make a great impression. Us this as your opportunity to earn their trust so that in the future they not only visit your blog but that open your e-mails and take action.

Here are some more examples of things you could use as lead magnets:

- Audio or Video info on how to do something (How to...)
- List of resources for a specific topic (70+ Places to...)
- How you did something great (How I improved my marathon time by...)
- Etc

Think outside the box, be creative, and challenge yourself to find new ways to provide people with something of immense value.

Drive Traffic

Now that you've set up your blog and some of the other necessary elements to be successful (E-mail list, lead magnet) it's time to go out and build an audience.

You are going to want to find as many people as possible that are already interested in your topic to connect with. Getting traffic is something that anyone who has a blog (or any website for that matter) struggles with.

The key is to not only get people to your site, but to get the right people to your site. You want to build a long-term passionate audience that will not only enjoy your content but will share it with other like-minded people.

This chapter is to help strategize on how to get traffic to your site.

Before I share with you what I think are the top ways to get traffic and build an audience, I want to cover 3 things I think you should specifically *not* do.

Don't Rely On Google

It's tempting to focus your writing/blogging on things like keyword research so that you can rank high in search engines like Google. There are a lot of problems that come with this strategy however.

One of those problems is that Google and the other major search engines are constantly changing the algorithm they use to determine your ranking. So, you can end up spending a lot of time jumping through hoops only to lose your ranking (and traffic) overnight.

This has happened to a lot of people in the past.

Another problem is that you end up writing your content for the search engines instead of your readers. You want your readers to love your content and share it with others who have similar interests. Deciding what to write by focusing on getting search engine traffic isn't a good long-term strategy.

Instead, just focus on writing great content. If people like it, you will still end up ranking high for the topic and search terms that apply to your blog.

NOTE: I mention using Google Keyword tools elsewhere in this and other books I've written. I want to make sure I don't sound like I'm giving you contradicting advice. I am all for using keyword tools to do research from a big picture standpoint. I just don't think you should try to use that as your primary source of traffic by writing content catering to those keyword results.

Don't Spend Money on Ads

Although some gurus out there preach that you should go out and start paying for traffic by running ads, I really think that you should focus on free organic traffic from sources that match your target demographic. This is especially true when you are first getting started.

It can get very expensive trying to get people to your site by paying for ads or competing for keywords. People are tempted to do this since it requires less work and can literally get you traffic overnight. Don't looks for the easy way out.

The reason this could be a problem is that unless you have a long track record with your blog and have already successfully grown your user base, monetized, and taken care of all the other aspects of your blog, paying for ads will likely not help you much.

Put in the time and work upfront to build an organic user base before you ever consider paying for ads.

Don't Do Anything Morally Questionable

There are a lot of strategies and tactics out there that are very questionable if not flat out unethical. There are even so called "gurus" out there that sell you on crazy ways to grow your blog. These can include anything from ways to trick the search engines, spam people, or other hair brained schemes I haven't even thought of yet.

People looking for a quick way to make a buck usually lose in the long-term. If you do anything against the rules with one of the search engines, you'll regret it. The same goes for any monetization strategy.

If you try and scam people, you'll regret it.

Instead, focus on the effective and honest ways to grow your business and make your blog be so valuable to people that making money is never an issue in the future.

Great Sources Of Traffic

Now that you have all the basics down and are ready to get some readers, let's take a closer look at places you can get additional traffic.

Social Media

One of the best sources of traffic for a new blog is social media. This includes Facebook, Twitter, Pinterest, and more. For the purposes of this book, I am going to be focusing on the big one, Twitter. Facebook, and Pinterest should also be able to provide you with a ton of great focused traffic if you use them similarly to how you will use Twitter.

Twitter

Here is a great way you can get awesome traffic from Twitter with just a few minutes of work each day.

First, go ahead and create an account on Twitter. Before you get started trying to get traffic from Twitter, make sure your profile looks good. Don't leave the default graphics on your profile, for example.

Change your profile picture and background to match your website. This will make it clear that your Twitter account is an extension of your blog. This will help you build trust on Twitter and make you look like a professional. Also, make sure your bio is clear about the value you intend to bring along with a link to your blog.

Next, go on Twitter and find people that are very popular in the topic you have chosen to start a blog about.

For example, if you are blogging about fitness, find the Twitter account of an already popular authority figure that has an audience similar to the audience you want to build. If your blog is about fitness for men, find someone already popular in that space.

Then go through and start following people that are following that authority figure. After all, if they are following that authority figure they obviously have enough interested in the topic to seek out and follow that person.

Once you start following people, you'll notice that some will start to follow you back. These people are prime candidates to be exposed to your brand so that they can someday become members of your audience.

Once you start getting more and more followers, you can even double back and unfollow those that didn't decide to start following you in return. If you don't want to waste the time on it, there are even paid services you can use for a few bucks a month to unfollow people who don't follow you within a certain amount of time.

If you do this on a consistent basis you should end up with an account that has thousands of people following you that are interested in your niche. That's when you focus on converting them to members of your audience.

How do you do that?

In order to take Twitter followers and make then engaged members of your audience you need to do two things. They are:

Engage them

Take the time to show that you are human by having conversations with people. If they ask a question, answer it. Comment on things they post. Be all around helpful and treat them like you would one of your friends.

As you start to build relationships with people on Twitter you'll notice a few things starting to happen. One of those things is that people will look to you for info on certain topics. You will slowly start to be seen as an authority, which is exactly what you want.

Another thing that will happen is other people who don't currently follow you will start seeing your tweets and then they can start to follow you. The reach you have on Twitter will grow faster and faster as you continue to build relationships with people.

Post Links to Great Content

The other tactic you need to take advantage of on Twitter is to post links to your blog when you have helpful information to share. For example, you just wrote and posted a 4,000-word article to your blog about how to do something that you think your audience would find useful.

That is a perfect time to send a tweet letting everyone know about your article. It also helps to give your article a title that is very catchy or describes the value that the reader will get from it so that people feel inclined to click on it.

Since there is a lot of "noise" on Twitter, you'll likely have to send this tweet several times over the course of a couple days to make sure people see it.

You can also do this with older articles from your blog as long as the content is still timely.

For example, if you wrote a great article on your fitness blog about losing weight after the holidays last year that you feel nobody saw since you had so little traffic at that point, feel free to share it again this year after the holidays.

This isn't a sales pitch and all your doing is linking to a helpful article. People will actually appreciate this, which leads to you getting a new reader.

Make sure that your article makes it easy for people to subscribe to your e-mail list, too. I always include a link at the bottom of the article so someone visiting for the first time gets a chance to subscribe.

Chapter 5 The Dashboard

Almost everyone wants to start writing immediately and posting their stuff on their blogs and websites. To get you started, there are a few things to learn about the Dashboard.

Think of the Dashboard like the command center of your website. This is where you can change the look and feel of your site, decide who can post things, who can comment, you can modify the way the site looks-everything!

In this section, we will explore some of the most important functions that are required to start up your website or blog. Remember that a good way to learn and remember the features of the Dashboard is to physically practice it while you read this chapter. Only then will you be able to understand the many functions of the site and work towards creating a blog or website that is intuitive, exciting and easy to navigate.

User Profile

When you click on it, the screen will bring you to a list of users that are using the account. There could multiple users assigned to the site, but there can only be one or two administrators. Multiple users for a site means that more than one person has access to the site. However, as the administrator of the site, you will be able to control what other users can or cannot do. You can assign roles such as Contributor, Author, Editor, Administrator or Follower. Each of these titles has its specific roles.

For example, the Contributor enables a person to only contribute content, but they are unable to approve or delete other content. The Author can only accept and edit content but cannot change the appearance of the site. The Administrator can do all of the above and have total control of the site. As the website owner, you get to decide who can have access to what segments on your site.

The Appearance Screen

The Appearance is where you bring life to your site. Depending on what you want your site to do, there are several themes that you can use to completely change the look of your site. These themes are designed by Wordpress developers and Wordpress users, and you can choose from thousands of themes some free whereas some are paid themes.

Each theme shown under the Appearance section is built to cater to a particular need for the user. For example, some themes are built to cater to a business type of site whereas some themes are made to feature photographs and pictures; some themes are built to feature fashion and online retail whereas some are built to hold writing and poetry or long articles.

To change the appearance of your site, all you need to do is click on a theme can click Purchase (if it is a paid theme) or Activate (if it is a free theme).

Not sure if you want the theme yet? Well, all you need to do is click on Preview to see how your site information fits in with the theme.

That's why it is a good to have at least some information or first post on your site before you change themes and the appearance of your site. Keep in mind that you would want to align the appearance of your site with the same branding that your business uses. Your online persona has to be the same with all the other marketing angles that you employ for your communications and marketing methods. The same goes for your personal blog.

Writing & Managing Posts

Posts are what make up the bulk of the content on your site. From the Dashboard, you can see the Posts link. Hover your mouse to that link and these other links will show up:

All Post

Add New

Categories

Tags

Copy a Post

These links are pretty self-explanatory, and you can use these various links help you create and manage your posts. DO not feel intimidated by the 'Add New' screen. On the screen itself, there are various helpful hints such as 'insert a title here'. Fill in the blanks one by one and then also use the various tools that you can see above the title section. The bottom line is, if you can use Microsoft Word, then you definitely can use the Wordpress Add New post feature.

Once you are happy with the way your post looks, you can either preview it or click Publish to make it go live.

Adding Media to Posts

There are several ways in which you can use the Add Media function in the toolbar. This function allows you to add in images, sound clips, and even videos. You can also add media via the 'Insert Tweet,' 'Insert Youtube' or 'Insert from URL' function on the right panel when you click Add Media.

You can add new media by uploading the necessary images or videos by using the Upload function that is located on the top of the Add Media pop-up window. When you add the media you want, again you have options. Wordpress allows a beautiful way of displaying media, especially images via the 'Create Gallery' function.

In this function, you would be able to display media via Thumbnail Grid, Tiled Mosaic, Square Tiles, Circle, Tiled Columns of Slideshow. This is a great way of showcasing several images in a more systematic and organized way.

However, you can also just add in one image to your content if an image gallery is not what you want.

Planning your Website

Designing a website or a blog requires planning and it needs a robust and good plan. Although setting a website or blog through Wordpress is free, you'd still want something that is lasting and memorable even if this website or blog is for personal use. You will also want to decide if you would like hosting your own site using Wordpress.org or you'd rather use Wordpress.com.

One a piece of paper, just uses at least 20 minutes to get your Mission Statement out. You'd want to have a few things determined for your site, so you have the focus to your site and you know the content you want on it.

Here are a few things to establish:

What will you do with your site?

What kind of content do you want on it?

Who do you want to read this?

How often do you plan on posting and adding content?

Depending on what you site is supposed to do, you will need to consider what kind of information you are willing to share and post. You would also want to include some contact information so your visitors to your site can contact you-unless you don't want them to.

Comments

Some of the fun and interesting things about Wordpress is its comments feature. This feature allows visitors to leave comments on your posts, and you get to comment back as well! Visitors can also rate a post giving five stars if they like it! Comments and ratings help push your website up in Google's search rankings too.

As the administrator of the site, you get to comment back and moderate the comments. Comments are a great way to have a connection with the visitors of your site, so there's a back and forth of communication and discourse.

As the administrator, you do not have to comment on everything that everyone says on your site however it is imperative if it is critical to your postings and sites. Some comments are really worth responding to if they benefit your site.

Just take note that not everything you post will go well with your audience. Everyone has a different perspective of things and therefore, their outlook on the numerous posts you have on your site may not be the same as your viewpoint.

Instead of trying to pacify everyone on your site-don't. It'll only take up a lot of time, and sometimes, it can even lead to a full blown debate which you do not want to be in. Let everyone comment and like your posts and comment where necessary.

Choosing a Domain Extension

A domain extension is the three letters after a dot that you see on a website link. This works for both the .ORG or .COM Wordpress option.

Usually, when you open a WordPress site, you'll often have your site with a URL such as this: www.mynewsite.wordpress.com. To change this without the WordPress name in it, you would need to register your domain, and this usually means paying for the hosting which Wordpress provides.

But before you can choose your domain name, a word of advice-do not attempt to change your site to a fixed domain unless you are very sure of the direction of your site and the content.

There is no rush of changing your WordPress site to a domain. Because this domain is fixed, you cannot be changing it all the time and of course, there's the cost factor.

Make sure your WordPress site is in the niche you want to focus and concentrate on. Making your WordPress site a functional and revenue generating website requires critical research on your target keyword pool.

If you want a Business Website-if this site is for your business, then a good domain to register your site would be a DOT COM as in .com site, such as mynewsite.com.

If you want a Personal Website-Well it's your own personal site so go with whatever you want, but the most popular is, of course, .com.

A non-Profit Website-for a non-profit site, the best domain name would be a .ORG.

Information Website-a .info, of course, would be the best!

There are plenty of domain name extensions but the most popular ones are .com, .org, .net and .info. And these are easily picked up by Google.

Choosing the Right Domain Name

The domain name and the domain extension go hand in hand. Once you have decided on your domain extension, you need to figure out what you'd like to call your site which will be your domain. Your domain name is what your website's URL will consist of when someone types it in the browser's address bar.

Here are a few crucial points to consider when coming up with your Domain Name:

Matching Names: Essentially the name of your site as well as the URL must match.

Short: So it's easier to remember and can be typed into the browser

Consistent Branding: Your domain is a reflection of your brand. Keep it consistent and memorable.

Memorable: Well, a website must be easy to remember and memorable, so you want it to stick the first time when your visitors come to your site.

Catchy: It must be easy to pronounce and rolls of the tongue easily. Your domain name must also describe what you do.

Includes Keywords: Because you want it to be Search Engine Optimized.

Essentially you want it to be easy to remember and easy to type. Your domain name must correspond with what your business does or what your personal online agenda is for your site.

Chapter 6 Customizing Your Website's Appearance

Themes in Wordpress make it easier for your to jazz up your site especially when coding isn't your biggest advantage. By using WordPress themes, you already have a designed website at least 90% complete. All you need to make it your own is to personalize it.

Not sure if you want the theme yet? Well, all you need to do is click on Preview to see how your site information fits in with the theme. That's why it is a good to have at least some information or first post on your site before you change themes and the appearance of your site.

Having these first few pages and posts will give you a good idea how the theme you have chosen will eventually look and feel like once you have confirmed your choice. You get to see how the posts will look like when a reader visits your site, you will get to see how your homepage is, you will also get to see the sidebar, footer and header details and whether this matches with your look and feel objectives.

Customizing and Personalizing

To make your site 100% your own, you can choose to personalize and customize the theme. Usually, customization is done on the fonts, the colors, and other simple design elements without altering the layout of the site.

To customize the theme you have selected, you can go back to the Appearance section and choose the Customize link. Here, you have the option of doing a variety of things to your site to make it sync in with your branding needs. Usually, most themes allow you to change the logo, the colors and backgrounds, the fonts, the header image, the menus and the widgets.

In this chapter, we will look at the various ways in which you can customize your site based on what can be changed. If you are not experienced in coding, best to leave the customization to the selected options. But if you do know coding and can take your site's customization to another level then go ahead-there is no stopping you and the sky is the limit!

Widgets

You can find the widgets section under appearance as well. Depending on the theme you have chosen, you will have a selection of widgets to choose from. Most widgets are the same for most themes, and some are a few extra special ones based on the type of theme you have chosen. Widgets are preset elements that are added to a site to improve its functions and improve your website's capacity.

Some of the same widgets you will often find in most of these themes are such as Archives, Blog Stats, Calendar, Category Cloud, Facebook Page Plugin, Gallery, Gravatar, Image, Instagram, Milestone, Music Player and Twitter Timeline. Take note that widgets are not Plugins but they are elements that enhance your website and add more functionality. Widgets help with navigation and also to improve your connectivity to your social media. Widgets are extremely useful so you should add this to your site.

To add a widget, just go to the Widget section, click on Add a Widget. From then on, you can see a list of several widgets that you can add to your site. Click on the Widget you would like to add and then click 'Save & Publish.'

Menu

You can also change the Menu section of your website. Menus are a crucial element to any website. They offer a means of navigating your site and all of your content. You want your visitors to go through all your captivating content and how can they do it without knowing where to go and find your content? That is when the menus come into play. If your menus and navigation are hard, your visitors will find it hard to find your content, and this can lead to high bounce rates-which is the number of visitors to your site, how long they spend on it and how many posts they view before leaving.

Menus usually appear on the top of the site (because that's where people look first). Sometimes, you can find the menus at the site or even at the bottom. This is fine as long as you know what you want your visitors to focus on when they first come to your site.

Menus must include pages like 'About' 'Contact', 'Product', 'Services' as part of your primary menu. You can always remove or add pages to your menu according to what your site requires. Some menus and their placement on your site very much depend on your WordPress theme.

A good menu has several characteristics which are:

- concise and minimalistic

- represents of all your site's offerings

- very intuitive to use and easy to navigate around your site

Keep these elements in your mind when arranging and working on your menu and you will be okay.

Background

Now we come to the background section that you can change. Plenty of websites choose to have a white background as it is less distracting and keeps the focus on the main and relevant content. But then again, if you'd like to change the background of your website-go ahead!

Some media heavy websites such as those that host photography and portfolio have really fantastic backgrounds that work excellent with their products and services and branding.

A powerful background image will definitely send out a commanding visual cue to your site visitors. If a picture background is not something that is supported in your theme or you aren't a big fan of it, then opting for a plain color background that compliments your logo and your branding colors will do just fine. Just make sure that it emphasizes readability to your site.

Here are a few things to remember when you change your background:

- it must compliment the whole site

- it enhances readability and does not distract from the main focus of the site

- must not be confusing and is constant with the branding elements you have on your site

- do not use fancy animation as it is distracting

Plugins

Plugins are only available for Wordpress.org and are basically pieces of code that are written to perform a very specific function on your site. For example, the sharing plugin in added to your site allows you to share content across a variety of social platforms. The Wordpress community has developed a variety of Plugins that help in search engine optimization, enhancing the security of your site, maintaining extensive portfolios as well as including contact forms or inquiry forms.

Tags

Tags were similar to categories except these tags are specific to a post. Think of it like hashtagging an image on Instagram or on

Twitter. These tags aid your site's visitors in finding specific information and content on your site more easily.

Your Profile

Oh, how can we ever forget to talk about your profile page! Setting your Wordpress profile is really easy and one of the most natural things to complete when creating your website. You can always edit and change information on your Profile by going to your 'Edit your Profile' section found on the administrator screen at the top right corner of the screen. Here, give yourself a short description and also add in your social media links.

In the profile image, all you need to do is upload an image of yourself or your Logo, and this becomes your Gravatar account.

Under this section, you can also manage your Billing information- if you want to purchase any paid Widgets, Plugins or themes and you can also decide on the security for your site. Wordpress gives its users the option of generating a strong password so that your site is secure.

Bottom Line

Just start already! Sometimes the best way of learning about Wordpress is through trial and error. We all have many inhibitions when starting something new, but all these things are just opening up doors to failure.

Creating a website and generating revenue or getting your content out there in the fastest way possible is no small feat. It takes a lot of hard work, marketing and publicity to get people to know about your site and to get your products or services or just read what you have to say. But with WordPress, this seemingly hard task is made simple. For the next few chapters, you'll find more tips and tricks to get your website up and rolling and bringing the revenue.

Chapter 7 Blog Monetization – Digital Products (Ebooks)

Apart from selling ad space and engaging in affiliate marketing, another way of earning money with your blog is to sell digital products like eBooks and online courses. In fact, eBooks are like hot cakes now – every day, more and more people seek knowledge and if you package information that people seek in the form of an eBook, your readers would be happy to buy.

As a niche blogger, you understand your niche perfectly well – you know those pain points or problems that your readers might have. If you have really been paying attention to your audience, then you would have deduced some of their significant issues. Many times, you may find it hard to compile all the issues into a blog post, so, you might need to compile everything into an eBook.

How do you get eBook topic ideas?

The best way to get eBook topic ideas is to visit Amazon.com, then go to the books/Kindle section. Scroll through the section where you find books related to your niche. Look at the books that are already selling there. Read the reviews left on the books and see what people that have bought the books in the past are saying. Take note of the negative reviews so you can address them in your book.

A platform like Amazon, for instance, allows you to look through the first few pages of a book published on its platform. You can exploit that feature and look at the table of contents of some of the books that have been published in your niche. Use the information you get to form the table of contents for your eBook.

With the table of contents in your hands, you could proceed to start writing your eBook. Make sure that the eBook contains valuable information such that after reading, your readers could say, "wow, I have learned a lot from this."

If you do not have the time to sit and write or if you cannot write lengthy eBooks, you could hire ghostwriters on freelance platforms like Fiverr.com and Upwork.com to help you write an eBook. Usually, you would need to provide the ghostwriter with an outline and discuss other details of the eBook with them.

After writing and publishing your eBook on platforms like Amazon.com and other self-publishing platforms, then it is time to start aggressive marketing of the eBook. You could create a post on your blog to create awareness for the eBook. You could offer the eBook at a discount price for your readers – then ask them to drop a review after reading the book. The reviews will help to improve the ranking of the book and make other people want to read it as well.

Remember, when it comes to making money with eBooks, one book is not enough – you must write as many books as possible.

To start seeing reasonable income, you need to have at least five (5) books, and you must market them aggressively to your audience. Since each of the books would be in your niche, you need to link them all up so that customers who buy one could buy the rest of the books.

For each sale of your eBook you record, Amazon takes some part of the money and pay you the rest after a specific period. If you want to avoid this commission that Amazon takes, then you could consider hosting your eBook on your server – then sell it directly on your blog. For this to work, you need to have a payment processor like PayPal or a merchant account.

Once a customer buys the eBook directly from your blog, and you confirm their payment, send them a download link to their eBook. To make the eBook readable on many platforms, convert it into ePub, PDF, Mobi, or any of the other popular eBook formats. You could never go wrong with selling your eBook directly on your platform as you get to keep all the money.

Asides from selling eBook, you could create video courses and sell to your readers. The process is basically the same as that of producing an eBook. You could host the video course directly on your blog and sell to your readers, or you could host it on platforms like udemy.com Lynda.com, etc.

If you do not want to create courses or eBook, you could consider creating a members-only section on your blog. This area will contain gated content or exclusive information that will only be made available to those who pay a subscription fee.

To attract people to join the members-only section, you need to ensure that the general sections on your blog contain valuable information. This way, readers would be longing to see what's in the gated area. It is fundamental human nature – we are always interested or curious to know what's behind the veil. Now, you need to exploit this human nature and make money.

Remember, if people join your members-only section and find out that the information there is something basic they could find elsewhere, they would leave, and that would make your audience displeased. So, you should only create a members-only section if you genuinely have information which you think should not be shared for free.

If you decide to create a members-only section, people could try to guilt-trip you into making everything free. Those are people who think information shouldn't be worth anything. Meanwhile, those same people go to college and pay huge money for the same information. In essence, if you have something of value, don't be shy or guilt-tripped into giving it out for free.

Those who know the value of information will pay anything to have it. If anyone doubts the importance of information and the need for it to be monetized, then that person is not your ideal client anyway, and you should not be worrying yourself with such people. You should be more interested in those who place a premium on valuable information and make sure you provide them with real value.

In this chapter, we have just summarized some passive income methods you could leverage and make money on your blog.

Email marketing to sell more

No matter what you are selling on your blog, you need to grow an email list – your email subscribers are like your loyal customers – you could market any product or service to them, and they would buy. In the online business scene, it is often said that money is in the list and that's true. If you know how to leverage your list, then you can make money selling just anything.

Why is email list so important?

For you to understand why a list is essential, let's analyze how the world of business and sales have evolved over the past years. In the past, a company only needed to develop a good product, then send salespeople to market the products. Those days, customers could buy any product as long as the salesman selling the product is convincing enough.

However, a lot has changed today – the average customer now has a lot of options to choose from. In fact, they are just a Google search away from finding the right products that would solve their problems. In such a world where there are thousands of other people selling the same product that you sell or who offer the same service that you provide, how do you convince the average customer to patronize you and leave your competition? The answer is simple – you need to connect with the customer emotionally.

How do you connect emotionally with the customer? First, you need to understand that today's average customer buys based on emotions and justify logically. So, to make them buy from you, you need to excite them and make them feel emotionally connected to both your product and you as a brand. The only way you could do that is by befriending and communicating with them as friends.

When you constantly communicate with your prospects, readers, or potential customers, the propinquity effect will take its course and make them want to patronize anything you are selling. Apart from creating blog posts, you could communicate with your audience through emails.

With the right lead generation strategy, you could collect the emails of your readers and make sure that you send them the right emails. With the right emails, you could turn your followers or readers into loyal customers who would buy your products and continue to read your blogs.

Having a blog makes email marketing so easy – because you already have an audience – you need to nurture them with emails and warm them up about a product, then market the product to them. Usually, the first stage in email marketing is to acquire a huge audience which could be passed through an autoresponder.

Then the second stage is to use an autoresponder to warm up the vast audience and narrowly segment your list into those who might need your product immediately and those who might need it later. Continue to use a series of email swipes to warm up the subscribers until they are finally ready to buy and then market a product to them. This whole process usually takes time – from the first time that subscribers join your list to the time they are ready to buy. Research shows that it takes up to 7 contacts for a subscriber to be prepared to buy. This means you need to send messages to your potential customers many times before they are finally ready to buy.

Let's get practical

Let's assume that you have created an eBook, and you want to use email marketing to promote and sell this eBook. Here are the steps you need to take:

1. First, you need to use something to attract your potential customers to join your email list. Remember, the fact that someone reads your blog posts does not make the person your customer. At most, the person is just a potential customer, and you need to lure them into joining your email list so you could convert them into customers.

To get your readers to join your email list, you need to use something to lure them. For instance, create a free eBook lead magnet or trip wire and offer it to your readers. It could be a short read that would make them salivate and want more.

The lead magnet or tripwire has to be very captivating so that the reader would be asking for more after reading. The free lead magnet is to prepare the reader to buy the paid eBook or to leave their email in order to receive more information on how to get the paid offer.

2. After creating the lead magnet, make a post on your blog and offer it your readers.

3. Create a landing page using ClickFunnels or any of the other autoresponders like MailChimp. Once a potential subscriber submits their email to enable them to download the free eBook or offer, send them a "thank you" message and a link to download their free lead magnet.

4. Now that you have their email; use a series of well-crafted email swipes to inform and educate them about the paid eBook which you want them to buy. Tell them the benefits of the product, and why they need to buy it. Your reasons should be strong enough to make the individual decide to buy. Also, you could include social proofs to further convince prospective customers.

5. Once you have warmed up your leads for some time, introduce them to the product you want to sell to them.

The above approach works like a charm because even if the subscribers do not buy the immediate product you are marketing to them, you still have their email and you could sell other products to them later.

No matter what you are selling on your blog, email marketing will always prove important, and if you learn how to use it well, you will be miles ahead of your competition.

Chapter 8 Monetizing Through Sponsored Posts

Sponsored posts are one of the quickest methods of making money from your blog. Sponsored content is content that you are being paid to write or come up with by a company or a brand, which means that the content you create will have to be promoting a particular brand or service offered by the company in question. Sponsored content differentiates itself from marketing through one simple aspect – you are paid for the content you create, as opposed to relying on possibly generating an income based on the number of clicks or sales.

Introducing your readers to new products or services that they may not already be aware of is one way of providing value to your readers, but the trick is here to create content that is top-notch and honest at the same time without compromising the credibility of your blog.

When it comes to sponsored posts, you may be tempted to take on as many as possible because you are guaranteed a payment for each one, but cool your jets and try to avoid doing so, because a blog that has too many sponsored brands can be a turn off for a lot of readers. They will begin to doubt if they can really trust what your blog is saying if they feel you are just creating these sponsored posts for the sake of the money. Be savvy and be smart and selective about the kind of sponsored posts and campaigns you want to take on and limit the number of brands you commit to at any given time. Even though your content is being paid for by the sponsor for you to spin some positive light on it, it should still hold a genuine voice to it and not come across as fake to your readers. Before you hit the publish button, ask yourself - if you were reading your post from a third-party point of view, would it be convincing enough?

What Is the Earning Potential with Sponsored Content?

You need to know what your blog is worth. Earnings from a sponsored post can vary depending on the company and brand in question, but it is also important for you as a blogger to know what the value of your blog is. If your blog has been around for a long time, for example, and has developed a strong following with hits on the site every day, you have more bargaining power which will allow you to negotiate a better deal for your sponsored content.

Why Sponsored Posts Are an Awesome Revenue Generating Tool

With the rise of influencers online, companies realize the value of purchasing sponsored posts and are constantly on the lookout for influencers and bloggers to work with. Having a company featured on a blog is a great way to boost sales, and for this reason, it is a great way for bloggers to take this opportunity to make some money if they have a blog space to offer.

What makes sponsored posts so great is that you do not have to invest too much time or effort into it. In fact, it is quite possibly easier than a lot of other types of campaigns which can be more demanding and cost a lot more money. Sponsored posts are easy.

In contrast with affiliate marketing, one of the most exciting things about sponsored posts for bloggers is that they are paid more or less immediately. This may vary depending on the sponsor in question, of course, as some sponsors will prefer to pay up front and others may opt for payment only after you have published a post on them. Still, it is a lot faster than affiliate marketing and advertising, and the pay here can be pretty good depending on how popular your blog may be and how much traffic it generates on a daily basis. It is a quicker option to monetizing your blog compared to a lot of other monetizing efforts.

How to Secure Sponsored Posts on Your Blog

If you do not already have companies who are queuing up to get sponsored on your blog, then you need to be proactive and start approaching companies that you would like to work with and convince them why it would be a great idea to collaborate with your blog. If you are worried about whether your blog needs to be amazingly popular or have a high volume of traffic before companies and brands will even consider working with you, don't worry. As long as you can produce great content of value, that is going to be what matters the most.

When presenting your pitch to these companies, be specific about what the company or brand can expect if they decide to work with you. Tell them your ideas with enthusiasm and give them as much detail as possible to really show it is going to be well worth their time and money to secure a sponsored post on your blog. Tell them what you plan to write, who your readers are and what they want, how much traffic your blog generates, be as specific as possible and spare no detail.

Do not be afraid to show your creativity when trying to convince companies and brands to work with your blog. Creativity shows that you think outside the box and you are all about ideas. It is ideas with a creative spark that is going to drive an interest towards a product or service. Show the companies or brands that you hope to work with what you can do for them, and they will be more than interested in teaming up with your blog for a sponsored post or two. Maybe even more.

The Types of Sponsored Post Options to Work With

The types of sponsored post options that bloggers would have to work with are sponsored posts that have access to the readers and sponsored posts which are just a link to the blog or website. The type of sponsored content would depend on the company or brand's preference and what they think would work best for them.

Sponsored content that has access to readers would depend on the type of influence your blog has. The more influence a blog has, the more likely the company is to decide on this route when it comes to post sponsorship. Sponsored content that works with just a link would depend on how much authority a blog's domain has. The higher the domain authority, the more opportunities your blog will have. Which is why it is important to pitch as many details as possible about your blog to the company or brand you hope to work with so they can make an informed decision and get the most out of their sponsored post collaboration with your blog.

Chapter 9 Website Flipping

Website flipping is similar to domain flipping, but what is being flipped is a website instead. There are a few things that differentiate domain flipping from website flipping, and that is with domain flipping there is no need to enhance the domain. Unlike website flipping, you would need to make a significant investment in time and creative resources to turn a website into a high-value asset.

The business of website flipping is a lucrative one no doubt, but you will need keen insight and proper research to make it big in this field. There are those who have done it and have been very successful at it. Some websites have been flipped and sold for as much as 4,000% more than the original amount.

To start trading in websites, you must think "value." That's the only way to get the maximum return on your investment. If you have gone through SEO consultancy in the web design section, you would understand what value is to a website. I will advise you check it out but just so you have an idea, the important attributes of a high-value website is its SEO and backlinks.

What is its SEO program like? How many reputable backlinks redirect to it. These factors determine the value of a website.

Getting Started

When starting out in website flipping, I advise you start small. Make your investment in bits and learn as you go along. There is no need to hurry, there are over 300,000 websites registered daily so there are always good bargains to pick from.

THIS IS THE CATCH; people set up websites for various reasons, if that purpose is not achieved, they tend to abandon the project. You can get access to their website if they abandon it and it expires, or you can purchase it from them for a small fee. You need to be very business savvy and have a keen eye to make money here. You also have to be ready to research extensively to determine the value of a prospect and also to develop the ones in your portfolio so that they attract good value.

These websites can be bought by you for peanuts and then sold for hundreds if not thousands of dollars. Because new businesses are always looking for popular websites and domains, you can cash in on this and make some good money for yourself. Your responsibility is to find good websites, make them yours for peanuts, develop them extensively, and then sell to eager buyers.

With website flipping, you have to dedicate yourself to understanding the market; the niche that is fast selling, how to generate traffic, the best SEO technique to use, how to implement backlinks, and finally the design.

You may be tempted to want to build a website from scratch but I would advise against that for obvious reasons. It is my opinion that you want to develop a business model that has a good turnover rate, right? If this is the case, and it should be, the amount of time and resources it will take to build a site from scratch and develop it to the point where it can command a fair value is quite long. You could be at it for a year or more.

So what is the best approach? I will show you how you can purchase websites with some value for cheap, how to develop them, and then how to sell them for a high return.

Finding the Right Website

Deciding on the right website to purchase for flipping is essential to your success in this business.

Pick a Niche: The niche you decide on is also an important factor to consider. The highest grossing niches are health and fitness, sports and lifestyle. This is not to say that the other niches aren't profitable, but these are the ones that have brought good returns on investment in the shortest possible time.

Research: This is something you should be doing throughout your sojourn in this business. It may get easier over time but it does not stop, so get used to it. There are a few things you must keep in mind when researching websites. Your research will always take two forms. First, you have to find out the best website that is cheap, and secondly, you need to learn how to develop the website to the point where it can give you more value.

The best place to look when researching websites is on the Internet. Search Google for high traffic niches and go far into the

10th to 20th page to look in for potential prospects. If you find something you like, check the contact us page and contact the owner.

Note: there are penalized websites that cost next to nothing that you can also make an investment into and revamp for a good sale. I will discuss that later.

Avoid Scams: There are lots of scams on the Internet. If you sense anything shady about the website or its promoter, I will advise that you back out of the deal.

Marketing Your Website

After developing your new website, you will need to find a way to sell it for profit. There are several online platforms that cater to these sorts of things. Let us take a look at some of them. You can also find great bargains for websites on these platforms. Just look out and take the points we have listed above into consideration.

Below are some of the best places to start your website flipping venture.

1. *Flippa Marketplace:* Flippa is the best marketplace for trading websites and apps. It is one of the most popular platforms in the website auction space.

Most people come here to spend money. About 40% of visitors end up making trades. Your websites will have the best visibility here.

2. *Sedo Website Marketplace:* Sedo is one of the leading website trading marketplaces available. Sedo has over 2 million member accounts from around the world, all trading in websites and domain names. There is a huge market for your website here.

Sedo connects buyers with sellers to create an easy and smooth transaction experience. With over 18 million websites on sale, Sedo is the largest marketplace for websites.

3. *Website Broker:* Website Broker is a marketplace primarily designed to trade websites. In spite of this, domains are also traded on the platform. This is a great place to advertise your website. Sometimes you can cash in on a good bargain here. People are constantly advertising their websites on this platform.

4. *EBay:* eBay is one of the best places to sell websites online. You can find cheap websites here too. People are always looking to flip their websites and on a good day, you can strike a bargain. Just make sure that you do your homework before consenting to a transaction.

5. *Brand Bucket:* The brand bucket is one of the very popular platforms for website flipping. They only trade in quality, unique and high-valued websites. Most

websites on Brand Bucket attract prices in the thousands of dollars. This is one of the best platforms to trade websites. The opportunity for profits here is huge.

Key Points

Trading websites can be a little risky but it is highly profitable. It requires patience and tack to make it big here. Conduct your due diligence and make sure you have a written down objectives for any web asset you acquire. This will help you chart a roadmap on how to go about your investment.

To successfully trade in websites profitably, you will need to make some major investments. But not to worry, it will pay off if you apply the strategies I have taught here. The profit margins in website flipping are usually quite high, so what you require to at least break even is just one sale.

It is important to practice money management skills as well. Take it slow, start small. Once you have made a few trades and have started to gain practical experience, you can then move on to bigger turf.

Chapter 10 Listicle Blogging

Studies have shown that when people search for information, they prefer to read information that is presented in a step by step format, such as a list. It is believed that this format allows for easy perusal and digestion of the information. In fact, the title of this book is written in a listicle format.

Instruction specialist Abreena Tompkins conducted a research analysis about online learning and concluded that information grouped in parcels of three or five can better help people absorb information faster.

How is Money Made?

Like normal blogging, you can make passive income from advertising, affiliate marketing, and most of all, from selling a product or service.

The major selling point of a listicle blog is the catchy nature of it. For instance; you must have seen articles that are titled similar to the following:

15 Top Reasons to Visit Brazil.

7 Mistakes Most Bloggers Make.

5 Reasons to Use Listicle Blogging.

What emotions do these titles cause the reader to feel? Curiosity. You want to find out what the writer has in store. It also tells you what to expect; if there are seven mistakes bloggers are making, then you know when the list of mistakes are going to end; you can estimate how much time it will take you to get through the article, and how much information you will have to process. Listicle blogging is one of the fastest growing blogging niches.

Creating Your Listicle

In quick steps, we shall be examining 7 rules to follow when setting up a listicle blog.

1. Pick your topics carefully. Ensure you have adequate information and resources on whatever topic you choose to write on. It is advisable that you think broadly about the information you want to put out as you need to make your post clear and concise. Be sure to pick unique and interesting topics or elements, topics that your readers may not know about or are interested in knowing more about. Mention new ideas in your posts so your readers do not get bored.

2. When you have picked your topic and have adequate information, you should begin as planned but still be responsive to change. For example, if you initially set out to write about 10 great ideas but later found more resources such that you can now write 30 ideas, then it is better to change the plan and write about the 30 ideas instead. Studies conducted by the

industry-leader Moz on different types of content that generated backlinks and social shares revealed that long form content (articles longer than 1000 words) received more shares and links than shorter-form content. This was especially true when the larger content was more detailed and easy to follow.

3. Choose the format for your blog. There are three main formats, namely:

Ranking: This process determines the position of items on the list. The list should be based on merit, or it can take the shape of a hierarchy (e.g. from worst to best), or deadliest, or most interesting, or least creepy, etc.

List Theme: You can write about a particular subject of appeal, but make sure that it has a theme. Let the theme reflect the essence of the article.

Random list: Lacking in both theme or ranking, this is where you just throw ideas around and leave the readers to draw their own conclusions. This is best left to a good writer as it can sometimes lead the reader to become irritated by the lack of conclusions.

4. Write with the conscious intent to engage. Content is still the main selling point. Let your writing style be catchy, witty and informative. Use pictures to better tell your story. Post articles that get people excited and motivated. You can also share an

inspirational post on your listicle blog to motivate your readers.

5. Get controversial. You can choose a controversial topic and lure your audience in until they are emotionally engaged and begin to discuss the topic on your blog. But please be careful, do it in moderation as it may get you some backlash. Make sure YOU ARE PROPERLY AND FULLY EDUCATED ON THE TOPIC YOU CHOOSE TO TAKE ON.

6. Finally, keep your post titles short and sweet. This is one of the reasons Twitter has grown in popularity. An average internet user has an attention span of about 7.5 seconds. Most importantly, try to stay away from complex sounding titles that hamper your message and confuse your audience.

If you follow these steps, you are almost guaranteed success. Information on how to set up a blog has been extensively covered in the previous sections.

Chapter 11 How To Build An Email List

In this part, we will discuss how to manufacture an email list for your blog. On the off chance that you converse with any effective blogger, they will reveal to you the significance of having an email list. Having somebody's email will enable you to get in touch with them decisively. It is more probable for individuals to see and tap on your email than it is for them to get some answers concerning your most recent post online which implies you can't disregard the intensity of email and email promoting.

I will show you today how to gather messages through free traffic and pop-ups. Gathering email can be a tedious and a relentless procedure, yet significant.

I will do my best to make it straightforward for you. Keep in mind that building a decent email rundown will require some serious energy. Additionally, on the grounds that you have figured out how to gather 10,000 messages doesn't mean every one of them will tap on your email.

You have to ensure you are keeping your messages endorsers drawn in and hanging tight for the following email, which we will show you in this section. Ultimately, we will additionally direct you on the best way to make probably the most stunning messages. It will assist you with getting a higher snap through rate. Despite the fact that email promoting is fantastic, just 30% of individuals will peruse and click your email. We need to ensure we leave no stones unturned to do that and we need an elegantly composed email.

Gathering email

Toward the start of your blogging venture, you won't have a lot of cash to spend on publicizing. In this part we will keep everything free assets, which means, you won't need to pay a dime on gathering any messages. Presently there are two primary ways for you to acquire messages. The first is through a spring up.

You can utilize email assets like MailChimp to make a free spring up. What spring up will assist you with is the point at which somebody visits your site, they will get a major box directly before them. It will approach them to agree to accept our email list so they could get a free book or something along that line, as we discussed in the past part. Contingent upon your specialty give your perusers something of significant worth.

In case you're in the wellness Niche, you can offer your perusers free eBooks on the best way to put on muscle. Make sense of the considerable number of necessities and issues individuals have in your specialty. Make a free eBook or a cheat sheet and offer them for nothing. It is an unquestionable requirement have on your site. Odds are if individuals are on your site as of now, they won't falter to put their email in pop-ups with the expectation of complimentary data.

Presentation page

Presently the second method to gather messages is use something many refer to as a greeting page. When you join with mailchimp.com. which is allowed to utilize, you would then be able to begin making free greeting pages for your site. What point of arrival will do is help you gather messages through YouTube and different destinations. This is the place greeting pages come in.

Make your presentation page through mailchimp.com. At that point duplicate that connection and post it on your YouTube recordings and different sites on the web. Your presentation page will offer a blessing in return for their email. So on the off chance that you go on to wellness structures and specialty sites you can gradually include your point of arrival there to explicit individuals who are into your specialty. It is additionally an amazing path for you to gather messages on your YouTube recordings and other specialty related sites. You need your presentation page there ready for action. In the event that not, at that point you are passing up a great deal of free leads.

Making email

At long last, the fun part, how to make an email and how frequently you ought to send messages to your perusers. So the primary thing you have to ensure is that you have your appreciated email robotized. In case you're utilizing the administrations, we suggest mailchimp.com. You ought to have no issue mechanizing email since it is exceptionally direct.

At whatever point somebody agrees to accept your email list, the principal thing you have to do is ensure you are sending them the blessing you have guaranteed. Your "appreciated" email will be the main computerized email, ensure your "appreciated" email is sent following they enter their email. This would be your computerized email, since you have made you're free to email and mechanized it, we will presently discuss the recurrence and the sorts of email you ought to send your supporters.

As to rate, you ought to never email your perusers multiple times each week. There are two explanations behind it. To start with, you will have a lower shot of winding up in their spam email. Second, your perusers won't get irritated by your messages. Henceforth, they won't withdraw.

Concerning messages, update them about the most recent blog and the offshoot items you need to offer them two times every week. This is a decent principle guideline I like to live by. Not exclusively will they be locked in on the learning you give them, however they will probably turn into your clients. It won't resemble you're barraged with deals pitch constantly. Subsequent to attempting this for quite a long time and years, I can reveal to you this is the best technique for messaging your perusers.

On the off chance that you need to have a fruitful blog, you need your perusers connected with through email. You can lose online life following, yet the messages will live on for eternity. Some should think about email medieval, yet most organizations are running exclusively on email promoting. Try not to think little of the intensity of email advertising, particularly for bloggers. Utilize these techniques we just discussed in this section to gather messages. Try not to leave any stones unturned in the event that you need to make progress in blogging.

Chapter 12 Types of Blogs

There are thousands of blogs in existence today, and new ones are being created every hour. They all fall into different "types" or styles of blog, and while that makes things a little easier, there is still a bewildering array of these "types" for you to choose from. It is really important that you select the blog that suits you.

Let us look at some of these different types of blogs to help you decide on which one is going to suit your goals. As per usual in this business, you will notice there is some crossover between the types of blogs. But one thing every blog has in common is this simple fact: should you choose to do so, you can make money from it. Now, let us have a look at these different types.

The Personal Blog

These are the kind of blogs where people write about whatever their interests or hobbies are, or whatever floats the blogger's boat. It could be some aspect of daily life; it could be trees or politics, windmills or waterfalls, science or spirituality. The list is virtually endless.

These blogs exist usually because the writer wants to share his or her views on a particular topic, and impart what he or she identifies as useful information. If the blog strikes a chord with enough people, then it can be hugely successful, if we measure success by the number of followers or readers it attracts. Of course, there are some people who have no interest in monetizing their blog and that is fine.

Sometimes it is a pity because a blog like this with a large group of followers can be monetized quite successfully without intruding on the content, message, or core sense of the blog.

The Personal Brand Blog

The personal brand blog is the logical step for the hobbyist blogger mentioned above to graduate into something bigger, and something which will make him or her money. The purpose of this kind of blog is to build a relationship with the readers and ultimately generate leads for whatever it is the blog is trying to sell. This type of blog is perfect for building up a reputation for the blogger, to enhance his or her credibility as a leader in whatever niche or field he or she is writing in.

Coaches use this kind of blog, consultants, spiritual, or political leaders use this kind of blog as a vehicle to establish credibility. I would like to stress that the key here is building up relationships with its readers. On the back of this relationship, the blogger could sell himself as a coaching expert, or dabble in affiliate marketing, or sell his own training products or merchandise.

For those blogs interested in affiliate marketing you will hopefully have attracted a large enough audience in an appropriate niche to make your blog attractive to companies who use affiliate marketing. If you are selling your own products there will need to be plenty of them for you to make any decent money, and they will need to be high standard, whatever they are.

The Corporate Blog

We move from local to potentially global. By a corporate blog, I don't necessarily mean one conceived and maintained by big corporations like General Electric or Nike. I am talking about a blog whose focus and identity is wrapped up in its business. If you run a small company called **Bing-Bang Paper Products** and you've created a blog which is called **Bing-Bang News**, which is all about the merchandise sold by **Bing-Bang Paper Products**, then that would be classed as a corporate blog.

By the way, I made up **Bing-Bang Paper Products**, so don't try looking for them. Of course, there is a different look and feel to the huge corporate blogs of a company like General Electric, as opposed to a smaller company, but they have much in common. The blogs are written in order to attract people to the site, people who are interested in the products or services that are sold.

The primary goal of a blog like this is to capture leads or sales. The notion is that readers of the blog who are interested in the content will move on to become buyers or become converted to an email list or an offer. There is no pretense with these blogs, they are designed exactly as you would expect them to be. These blogs act as tightly focused sales funnels.

The Niche Blog

A niche is anything specialized that somebody is interested in. In a way, all blogs that focus on a narrow band of topics (even one topic) are niche. The most successful and engaging of these blogs are ones where the blogger is either passionate about his or her chosen subject, or very knowledgeable about it, or both. Within businesses, they can be tightly specialized, or they can be more generalized.

For example, somebody could write about his passion for shoes of all types, sizes, and styles. He might then decide to blog specifically about men's shoes.

The technical term for this is niching down, so the original blog deals with all shoes and the next blog niches down, or narrows the focus, by concentrating on just men's products. The blogger may want to niche down even further, by narrowing the focus to men's sports shoes, or niche further down by concentrating on shoes for athletes.

Maybe the blogger might want to niche down even further by focusing on shoes specifically designed for long-distance runners. I am sure the niche of long-distance running shoes has more subcategories to it, but I will leave the niching down right there because I think you get my point.

Case Study or Test Blogs

Case study blogs usually involve the blogger trying something out, it might be a new product or it might be a specific strategy relating to your niche. The blogger then reports in detail to his readers about his or her findings and conclusions. In the process, the blogger learns a great deal about whatever his subject matter and his audience is, and is able to provide useful insight on the subject at hand.

A good case study blog is extremely focused on its niche. For example, if you wrote a blog about pet grooming (a process that can be quite stressful for animals) you could try different techniques on pacifying various animals, and then report back. This kind of blogger must also stay extremely focused on the problems his audience are having.

It goes into great detail on exactly what it is the blogger did and the results he or she achieved. Well-presented and written case study blogs can provide bloggers with an air of authority.

Guest Blogging

As of recently in this book, we have talked about a ton of approaches to get traffic to your blog. The present section, we're going to discuss the granddaddy of all, visitor blogging. Posting your article on another person's blog, otherwise called visitor blogging is a standout amongst the most ideal ways for you to produce traffic to your blog.

Presently there are two or three things to recollect before you begin posting your online journals on other individuals' sites. The main thing you need to ensure is that you have a few online journals all alone website before you post on others. Let's be honest, nobody needs new bloggers to post on their site, get a few certifications and compose a superb blog or two develop a resume. When you've figured out how to post a few web journals all alone website, at that point you can begin reviewing visitor writes so as to produce more traffic and to get some reputation in your specialty.

The sooner you begin visitor blogging, the better it will be for your image. It will enable you to make more backlinks, yet it will likewise enable you to pull in more perusers to your blog. Another extraordinary thing about this strategy is that if the site you posted on gets new perusers, the odds of the new perusers to visit and turn into a peruser of your blog would be high. Presently you should simply discover individuals who will enable you to post on their site, that is the thing that we will show you in this part.

Specialty explicit

Before we move further into this part, we have to clear up a few things. In the event that you need to benefit from your visitor blogging tries, at that point you have to ensure that the site which you have chosen to visitor present on is connected on your specialty. It can't be "kind of" related with your specialty, it must be decisively identified with your specialty.

For example, on the off chance that your specialty is tied in with lifting weights, at that point you discover a yoga site searching for a visitor blogger, don't proceed to attempt and post on their webpage as you won't increase any traffic from it. Kindly remember this progression as it is basic for your achievement in the blogging scene. You won't win any new perusers from it. On the off chance that the "kind of" related site chooses to post your article on their site, they may lose a few perusers and you may likewise lose a great deal of regard in the blogging scene.

Discovering sites to post on

Before you feel free to discover locales to post on, ensure that the site you find is progressing admirably. The most ideal approach to see whether the sites are getting a ton of connected perusers is to perceive what number of social offers a particular article or the site is getting.

That is a standout amongst the most ideal approaches to see whether the site is a go-go or no-go. Beyond any doubt you can post it on every one of the spots conceivable yet this will just make you look frantic for traffic That isn't what you need to resemble in case you will have a long haul supported business. Presently there are a great deal of approaches to discover sites to post on, yet the best site is clearly Google.

Simply look "Present a visitor post." If you see a site in your specialty which is tolerating visitor posts, email them. It is as straightforward as it sounds. They may request that you send a connection to your ongoing post so ensure you are composing the most ideal articles.

Composing the post

When you at long last found your site to post your blog on and they have acknowledged you, it will be an ideal opportunity to compose the article. Contingent upon the webpage and their perusers, your composing must be at a similar dimension as the site you will be visitor blogging on. This will enable you to draw in more perusers to your blog.

So as to do that, you have to do look into about their site. Peruse every one of the articles you can on their site. At that point make sense of if their perusers are propelled level, amateurs or middle of the road. Since that will have a major effect in the rush hour gridlock, you will produce from your visitor post.

You would prefer not to compose a careful article on a novice's site. It will just make perusers neglect your articles. By and large ensure that you are obliging their gathering of people. Which means, you need to compose an essential article if their site is a fundamental site and the other way around.

Discover what is working

When you are doing your examination on the site, attempt to discover the most shared and the most seen post. That will enable you to make sense of what the group of onlookers needs. Attempt and compose a comparative post simply like the most prevalent one on their site. That will satisfy the site as they would get a ton of perspectives and offers. Likewise, this will help you massively support your blog consequently developing your business.

Keep in mind, when you have the chance to compose on another person's blog, it isn't about you or your image. You are composing as a visitor, helping the site get more perspectives and offers. Visitor blogging will enable you to produce more traffic to your blog, yet that ought not be your essential core interest.

In the event that you attempt and advance yourself in the visitor post, at that point odds of you landing more positions later on will be practically nothing. Trust me, you will get traffic from visitor posting however don't advance yourself on the article. That being stated, I trust you have delighted in this book so far as we are arriving at its finish.

Chapter 13 Types Of Content That Can Sky-Rocket Your Blog Traffic

There's no short cut to success. If you want to build a profitable blog, you have got to put in a lot of stellar content out there for your audience. Not just that, you have to diversify your content strategy to use different types of content formats that work. There are plenty of fresh and interesting ways to present your content and grow the blog. Don't know how?

Here's a list of different types of content that are proven to draw a large audience, increase engagement, boost SEO and help you build a solid brand.

1. How-to Posts

Everyone loves step-by-step how-to tutorials which make the process of learning something new or solving a problem fairly simple. Any solution showing a how-to post or video is a golden opportunity for attracting a targeted audience. If laid out in an easy-to-understand, step-by-step and detailed manner, these posts/videos perform extremely well and go viral really quick.

Pro Tip: Make it a long and detailed post, almost like a short report or book. It is great if you can include images or screenshots describing each step.

2. Latest News

You will not believe the number of pages that make money on the internet purely on shock value. Of course, unless your blog is an all-news blog, you can also use breaking news related to your industry in combination with other pieces of information.

The biggest advantage of breaking and latest news is that you do not have to create it from scratch. You just have to put together the most important bits of information and rewrite it. Lots of blog owners curate news pieces from other sources and link back to them.

People love to follow interesting or important pieces of information related to their industry or area of interest. It goes a long way in establishing your blog's credibility and authority, which is important if you want to get people to buy from you.

The way to get it right is by opting for quality over quantity. Do not populate your viral fed or blog with too many click-bait style breaking news pieces. Position yourself as an idea influencer in your industry. Offer only high value, useful and insightful content. You can either publish a piece of breaking news daily or create weekly/monthly news updates.

3. Infographics

Infographics are hugely popular, especially when it comes to social sharing. People love to share content that is presented in a comprehensive, yet condensed, format.

Human beings are wired to be attracted to anything that's presented in an easy-to-understand, visual format. We dig interactivity, research, and stats that are packaged in a more digestible form.

Creating appealing and share-worthy infographics is time-consuming. You can do it yourself using an app like Canva or Photoshop if you are more graphically inclined or you can hire someone from elance, Guru or oDesk to do it for you. Visual.ly is also a good place for getting started with infographics.

If you do not want to make your infographics from scratch, share existing ones. There are lots of handy infographics available to be embedded through a simple Google search. Just ensure you have the permission to use it, and credit it to the right source.

4. Lists

Again, it is no secret that people love lists, which explains the barrage of "10 best things to do" and "30 best places to head to" etc. on your social feed. Readers love content that is presented to them in a systematic, digestible and structured manner.

Can you really resist clicking on list-based headlines that sound interesting and informative? This is the classic go to post for any content creator or marketer.

There's a neat little trick to get these posts right. Start by introducing a problem. List possible solutions for the problem, and offer a strong, actionable conclusion that nudges the reader to act upon these solutions.

Provide value to the reader by making these list posts as detailed and comprehensive as possible. Most Important – be sure to give these posts attention-grabbing and nonmisleading headlines. Your "10 Good Content Formats" (even if exceptionally well-written) may not grab as many views as "10 Outrageously Successful Content Formats That You Aren't Using Yet." If you need people to be all ears to your message, convey it with a punch.

Pro Tip: do not just list all the points to read like a grocery list. Take the time to discuss each point, offer your own insights, present numbers and justify the item's inclusion in the list. For instance, if you are telling people Greece is one of the best places for destination weddings in 2017, tell them why too (number of tourist, great weather, visitor friendly conditions, easy laws, etc.). Always focus on offering a strong value proposition to your audience.

5. Round-Ups

Expert round-ups may seem easy because you are not creating the content yourself. However, it may take time and effort to put it all together.

Round-ups are nothing but posts where several experts in your subject share their number one tip or answer a focused question related to topic. For instance, if you are running a blog in the internet marketing domain, you may pose questions such as "What is your number one tip for growing social media followers or generating traffic for your blog?"

Round ups work because they are beneficial for everyone involved. Your readers get access to a whole list of expert tips. The influencers get to reinforce their expert status by sharing your post among their followers and readers. You get plenty of shares from different experts (imagine 20 different experts all sharing your posts among their followers to demonstrate that they have been featured as experts yet again).

However, it is not easy to put together a round-up. You need to approach influencers and get them to agree to be featured in the round-up. However, if you can pull off a few fantastic round-ups, you may manage to draw a swarm of blog traffic.

Some good tools for finding influencers in your niche are BuzzSumo, Traackr, Linkdex and more. You can also search on social media using popular hashtags or keywords related to your niche.

6. PowerPoint Presentations and Slides

This is a highly proven format that seldom goes wrong. It makes for a visual and interactive way to get across information to a focused audience. Slideshare is a great platform for sharing information in a slide show format.

Keep it a mix of information and entertainment. Do not make the readers feel like they are being held hostage in a boring meeting or the boardroom. Even the most serious topic can do with a dash of humor. This is a simple yet highly effective way to put across a ton of information in a quick, understandable format.

7. Case Studies

Case studies are a perfect way to flaunt your expertise in the industry. The ideal way is to take up something that you have worked on yourself. If you can present to your readers how a particular approach helped others meet their goals, etc., you will automatically appear more authoritative and credible to them. If you are selling a product or service on your blog, it is a good idea to include a case study about the value it offered someone. You are doing nothing but validating your product or reinforcing its merit.

A great case study is similar to a how to post, only more focused, insightful and detailed. Sum it up with the lessons readers can take back from it along with a powerful conclusion that gets them thinking. End with a strong call to action.

Pro tip: Do not simply rattle away facts and figures to appear intelligent. Weave the fact and figures into a story to make the case study more relatable and identifiable. Adding a human touch to it makes it more engaging than a clinical approach of merely rattling off facts.

8. Reviews

These are your manna from heaven where blog profits are concerned. Review-based posts are great for affiliate marketers promoting the products and services of others.

Richly written, pictorial and detailed reviews, which are presented in an easy to follow format are hugely lucrative.

Ensure the reviews are broken up into short paragraphs. Include lots of bullet points (pros and cons of a product or service), tables and visuals. Tables can be used to demonstrate what the product or service offers in comparison to similar products or services.

The ideal structure is beginning with an introduction, sharing your experience with the product (merits and demerits), and a conclusion (stating whether you would recommend the product to your readers). Summarize the key points of the review to facilitate quick reading for those who do not have much time at their disposal.

Finally, include a powerful call to action.

9. Guides, eBooks or Short Reports

If you think there is a huge need for detailed and lengthy information related to a particular area of your niche, go ahead and create a detailed guide or short report for it. These are more extensive in content and visuals than blog posts. You can offer your readers to download it in PDF format. What's more?

This can be a huge bait for getting interested readers to sign up for your email list. Enlist the assistance of a graphic designer to help you put together the layout and cover for the guide or report.

If you want to make the value proposition even more, create an entire eBook related to the topic. You will get ideas for the book simply by keeping your ears close to what your readers are saying. For instance, if you own a travel blog and keep posting about your global adventures, readers may ask you about how you manage to travel to so many destinations or your favorite tips for traveling cheap. This is a great opportunity to dive head on into creating an eBook about budget travel tips. You get the drift? Identify an area where people are desperately looking for information within your niche. It does not have to be a 200 page document. You can create a short eBooks with an eye-catching cover and gripping, valuable content. This is also an effective way to attract more readers, social media followers and subscribers.

10. Memes

Admit it, we have all shared memes that have made us laugh or touched us deeply. Memes are not just great for social sharing but also help your readers take a breather from more long-winded and serious content, and look at the lighter side of a situation.

Memes can be made without much time or effort using resources such as Meme Generator or Quick Meme. They can be customized for any subject or industry. If you want to put your point across in a smarter and more light hearted way, memes are the way to go.

Of course, they cannot be standalone pieces of content on your blog. However, they can be used for gaining some social media traction or complementing text posts.

To avoid any miscommunication or controversy, ensure that you do a little background research to understand the connotations attached to different characters and what they stand for. Do not blindly lift images to create memes without understanding the attached significance. The last thing you want is a backfired effort.

11. Interviews

Interviews are another great way to impress your audience. The more authoritative and influential your interviewee, the better it is for your blog credibility. Your followers/readers can learn a lot when it comes straight from the horse's mouth. Pick an important figure within your industry, and get them to feature for a full-length interview on your blog.

You can either do a video interview, a live podcast or send a list of questions for the person to answer in a textual format. Look at Mixergy for instance. The site is dedicated to interviewing accomplished people.

How do you go about conducting an interview?

Begin by introducing the expert. Highlight their accomplishments to make the prospect of listening to them attractive for readers.

Prepare a list of questions in advance by doing some background research about the experts. Of course, follow up questions will pop up throughout the interview. However, a set of prepared questions will lend it a structure. Conclude the interview by doing a quick summary of all the interesting and important things discussed in the interview. Offer your audience/readers a clear takeaway. Make a conclusion more urgent and actionable.

12. Printable Check Lists and To-Do Lists

This one sure makes the life of your readers easier by compiling all the scattered tasks or items into a single, organized list. It ensures that a task is done more efficiently, and nothing is left out. Wedding checklists, travel checklists, new baby checklists, blog creation checklist, etc., are extremely popular among their target audience.

Give your readers the option of saving these checklists in a printable PDF format. Checklists are great when it comes to getting readers to sign up for your mailing list.

13. Videos

Videos are a brilliant way to make your content both appealing and informative to your readers. Multiple studies have pointed to the fact that people register things more powerfully when they see it being done than simply reading about it.

Visuals strike a chord with your target audience and add variety to your content strategy. Social is becoming increasingly visual in nature. It is all about eye-catching visuals and slickly packaged, easy-to-follow videos. Also, YouTube is the world's second most widely used search engine, which gives you a fair idea about the amount of video content people are consuming.

Make videos that show off your blog's/brand's personality. It does not cost a lot to make basic, good quality videos. Use a smart phone for capturing a video, along with an editing software tool such as Camtasia.

Experiment with multiple video formats like screencasts (talking into the camera), fast paced videos or explainer videos. Keep it short, power-packed and to the point, since people do not really have the time to view videos that ramble endlessly. Plus, putting up your video on YouTube boosts your social signal with Google, who sees all the engagement as a validation of your content and popularity among readers.

Pro Tip: Give your videos a more well-rounded context by including a blog post or a video transcript (that viewers can later refer).

14. Spotlight Posts

People love human interest stories that relate to other people. When you create personal spotlight posts, you instantly engage followers emotionally. It makes the content more interesting and digestible for people. For instance, you can create a behind the scenes story featuring your employees or clients.

Make your blog more personal by showing your audience how it works. It will invariably make your brand appear more human, identifiable and approachable.

Chapter 14 Best Blogging Resources

Blogging is a business! If there is one thing you need to get from this book it's that treat your blog as a business and you will make money.

No business is run by just one person and blogging is no different. You'll need to manage your online empire with a range of resources from hosting your site to finding the best ways to put your products together.

I've referred to the resources I use throughout the book but wanted to include a resources page to put them all together in one spot. Some of the resources below require a subscription fee while others are free. Try out some of the free trials to make sure you like the service before putting any money down.

Hosting Providers

The first thing you need to do to set up your blog is to register with a hosting provider. Web hosts will hold your site on their tech hardware and make sure it's accessible to visitors. Most hosting providers charge between $2.99 to $10.99 per month for starter packages but pay attention to special features in each deal.

Blue Host is one of the most basic hosting providers. You won't get as good customer service as some of the others but it's hard to beat

Blue Host prices. A good low-cost option to try out blogging without committing too much money.

Host Gator is more expensive but offers a lot of extra features and is still inexpensive on a monthly basis. You'll get better customer service and website performance compared to the cheaper options.

GoDaddy is the most popular hosting provider and a good in-between choice compared to other options. You get all the customer service and features you need at a good starting price.

Plugins and Tools

Plugins and tools will help you run your blog without knowing a bunch of computer programming. They'll also help you manage your blog in the least amount of time possible.

HootSuite is my favorite social media management tool. Instead of spending an hour every day going to the different social media websites and sharing content, you link up all your accounts in Hootsuite and manage them all from one page. Social media traffic and sharing is a big part of blogging so this tool is a must.

Pretty Link makes the URLs to links on your blog...pretty, instead of a jumbled mess that scares off visitors. Pretty Link is a must for tracking clicks from your website to affiliates and products to make sure you are getting credit for your sales.

Fiverr is my go-to resource for outsourcing and small projects. Freelancers post projects they are willing to do, starting at $5 and up. It's a great site for testing out a freelancer's skills before you commit to a larger project. Fiverr is also a good place to offer your own projects for hire.

Ad Inserter is a plugin that allows you to customize a note to be placed on posts, pages or anywhere on your blog. Helpful for disclosures like affiliate advertising and other disclaimers.

Google AdSense plugin makes it easy to place your Adsense boxes on your blog with just a click.

GetResponse will help make email marketing a breeze with its automated process allowing you to send out series of emails to new subscribers.

BoardBooster is a must for managing your Pinterest account. I get thousands of visitors from Pinterest each month and know other bloggers that get tens of thousands from the social media site. BoardBooster makes it easier by letting you set your pins on an automatic loop so you don't have to go to the site every day to pin.

Canva is a design tool to help create cover and image graphics. Easy tool for feature images and product covers.

DepositPhotos is the site I use to find images for my blog. Don't make the mistake of thinking you can just download images for free from Google, it will get you in a lot of trouble and cost a lot of money. DepositPhotos is one of the least expensive image sources and typically runs special deals.

Affiliate Networks

CJ Affiliates is my favorite affiliate network and has a huge database of more than 3,000 advertisers. Quick paying and great publisher support.

FlexOffers was the first affiliate network I was on but takes longer to pay than some others. It's still a good network to be on and you'll find some advertisers that you won't get on other networks.

Amazon Associates is the site's affiliate network platform. Sign up and start linking Amazon products on your blog to receive a commission. Low commission rates but higher conversions than with other networks.

Self-Publishing Resources

<u>Ablurb</u> is a handy tool to create html for your Amazon description page including H-tags and bolded text. This will help get your books ranked and improve the SEO power on Amazon.

<u>Amazon Kindle Publishing</u> is where you'll go to publish your books on Kindle. Good reporting and an easy system to use.

<u>CreateSpace</u> is a print-on-demand service owned by Amazon. Upload your books to sell print versions directly on the Amazon page.

<u>ACX</u> is Audible…also owned by Amazon. It will take a little more work to convert your books to audio versions but it's well worth and your audiobook will be available next to other formats on Amazon.

Product Tools

Whether you need help creating or selling products, these tools will help you find what you need.

<u>Shopify</u> is one of the largest ecommerce platforms and offers several different solutions. I use it to sell printables and ebooks directly from my blogs. You can also set up a Shopify ecommerce store and sell directly from the page.

eReleases is a great press release provider to get the word out on your event or any large product launch.

Udemy is an online video education platform. Use it to launch your own courses or to learn how to do something by taking courses. The site regularly has offers for courses as low as $15 for hours of video learning. As an instructor you get 50% of the payout on courses Udemy sells and 97% of the payout on students you bring to the site.

Membership Sites

Running your own membership site is easy with the right software.

S2Member is the least expensive membership software because it offers a free version, though you will have show advertising. The Pro version is a better choice and only a one-time fee to include all the special features for launching your membership site.

Member Mouse offers better customer service and software updates on a monthly pay plan. It's less expensive to get started but charges every month rather than one-time. Some great additional features for your money.

Chapter 15 How to Use All These Methods

We are now going to talk about how to use all the methods listed in this book in order to get the best results possible. Even though we might have discussed every single topic step by step, it is crucial we teach you how to execute these strategies precisely. Don't worry it won't be overwhelming. We will make it easy for you just as we have done in this book so far.

We will show you what steps to take first and what steps to take at the end because there are some things we don't recommend you to do from the get-go and there are some other things we recommend you to do from the beginning. We will clear that up for you. All you need to do is follow the steps in this book in order to achieve great success with your blogging business.

However, doing these methods strategically is a different story. For instance, how can you post your very first article if you don't even have hosting or a domain?. That is just a mini example as to why it is essential to do these steps in a strategic manner. The truth is, this might be the most critical chapter in this book if you want to see results quickly. In the beginning, I knew all the steps on how to grow my blog all thanks to my cousin. However, I had no idea of how to execute them. With experience, I have learned. I can show you how to.

Step 1: Build your blog up

As simple as it sounds, you need to build your blog before you can try any unique methods. What I mean, don't try and do too much in a short amount of time. Build up your blog, focus on the basics before you can move into the advanced stuff. The basics include getting hosting and domain name, writing your first ten blogs and building as many backlinks as possible.

Don't even worry about creating affiliate links or guest posting, build up the base before you decide to take other steps. In the first month, you won't make a dime from your blogging business. More specifically, your job will be to write as many blogs as possible while creating as many backlinks and social media shares.

Building up your base will help you get some fame for your blog. Also if you can make YouTube videos, the video-sharing site will help you reach more people, our end goal in this first step. More importantly, try and collect as many emails as you can. That should be your first step in regards to your blogging business. One month of writing good content and obtaining as many emails as you can while creating more backlinks every day, and getting those social media shares. Think of month one as Chapter 2,3,4,6 and 7-8. These are the steps you need to take in the first month you start your blog.

Step 2: Making money

After you have managed to build up your blog, it will be time to make some money. This is a time when you will start looking into affiliate programs and start promoting them to make money. Figure out the top affiliate in your niche and start promoting those to make money.

You can also start looking into guest posting since you have managed to write up a couple of blog posts on your website. You have a resume, which means you can go ahead and start applying for guest posting. In the first month that you collected emails, you can now begin promoting your products and latest blog post to your readers through email using the strategy we talked about.

These steps are significant and you are required to make money so you don't stop building your blog. Your blog building never ends, which means creating backlinks, getting more social media shares and collecting more emails should be a day in and day out thing and not a one-month thing.

If you want to make $3,000 and beyond you need to keep growing your blog to keep people from leaving it. You need to keep building your blog every day. Once you get the ball rolling, you should have no problem getting more leads day in and day out. To do that, you need to create backlinks actively, collect as many emails as you can and to get social shares on forums and Facebook groups.

These are all the steps you need to take in order to get your first $3,000 a month income, make sure you do the steps in the strategic manner we just discussed in this chapter as it is crucial that you do so. By now you should have a great idea on how to make money on blogging. I do not doubt on you earning $3,000 a month from blogging if you follow the steps listed in this book. In the beginning, please don't try to experiment on anything.

Take all the steps listed in this book for optimal results. You can start experimenting once you start making money. This book was written for people who are looking to see fast income results from blogging. Remember this is not a book written for people to experiment and try new stuff. As we are getting close to the end of this book, I want to clarify a couple of things.

You will make money if you follow this book's advice. It could be $3,000 a month or $10,000 in 90 days. It just depends on your dedication, your ability to learn and how lucky you get. If you are serious about making money from blogging, you will need to follow this book step by step. You will have all the time in the world to experiment later on once you start generating income from your blog. To see fast results read this chapter very carefully and do what it says.

Chapter 16 Common mistakes

Business blogs are just as capable of, and in many instances more likely prone to, failure as personal blogs. In fact, over ninety percent of business blogs that go live on the internet end up failing. The reasons for the failure are generally the same. However, there are also some things that are specific to business blogs that can lead them to fail as well. Knowing what frequently leads to failure can often help you learn what to avoid and how to ensure you can avoid making common mistakes and therefore, can lead yourself to success in your business blogging.

Lost purpose

If all you are posting to your business blog are repurposed press releases, company news or glorified advertising copies, you are not going to be successful in reaching your customers. Your customers don't care about those things. Your customers want to be educated and informed about what you are selling them and information that relates to that. However, they don't want to be sold your product through your blog. Instead, post things that are going to let your customers know about things without making them feel that your goal is to sell them your product.

Don't believe in the power of blogging

If you begin a blog believing it is going to fail, then you might as well not even begin because it is going to fail. If you believe that you are not going to be successful, you are not going to be putting the work into the blog that it requires to be successful. Tell yourself that you are going to be able to succeed with a business blog and you are much more likely to put forth the effort that is required to be successful. You have already created a business; there is no reason you can't also create a blog.

No goals or strategy

Do you know what you are hoping to accomplish with your business blog or are you creating one because you know it has the potential to benefit your business? If you don't create any real goals for your business blog, it is not going to have a direction to grow in and isn't likely to get off the ground. Just like you needed to set goals for your business to succeed, your blog needs them too. Set goals that pertain to the number of people you want to reach and the time frame you want to reach them in and watch your business blog's success

No patience

If you are expecting your blog to bring in a whole bunch of new customers right away, you aren't going to see that. Having unrealistic expectations is more likely to leave you disappointed in how your blog is performing and, as a result is more likely to cause you to quit when you don't see instant results. Just like it took some time for your business to take off, you need to understand that it is going to take time for your blog to reach people. Instead of giving up after a few short months, commit to a time frame of at least a year before you tell yourself it isn't working and stop using your blog.

Nothing substantial

Just because your topic and title are appealing to the customer, it doesn't mean that your content is going to be automatically great. If your content is lacking substance or is full of errors and is hard to read, you aren't going to be able to maintain any readers. Ensure you are taking the time to edit and proofread what you are posting for its readability. On this note, you don't want to have content that is full of industry specific words and acronyms that your customers aren't going to know, and you also don't want to dumb things down to the point your customers are going to feel that you think they are uneducated.

Aren't giving opinions

Every blogger needs to be opinionated, and this extends to business bloggers. If you are stating facts without giving a true opinion of what you believe, your customers aren't going to be interested in reading what you are writing. For example, if you use a particular type of wood in all of your furniture, they want to know why you think it is the best. They don't only want the statistics about why it is best and the research backing it up; they want your opinions. Your opinions are what tell people they can trust you.

No updates

Coming up with fresh content for a business blog can be difficult. But if you aren't regularly updating your content, your readers aren't going to be loyal. Instead, they are going to go in search of another blog that is always posting new content. You want to be consistent in adding new blogs, and this is why it is recommended that business blogs keep their posts shorter, as it leaves more room to build off previous posts. Set a goal to post at least two blog posts a week to ensure that you are constantly providing new content, and you keep engaging your followers.

As you can tell, keeping a business blog appealing to your customers isn't the easiest job out there. However, if you use the tips in the previous chapter, and you are aware of the possible places you can fail that we covered in this chapter, you are much more likely to be successful at creating a blog that is beneficial to your business and encourages your customers to be long term followers.

Conclusion

Blogging is a great way to make money online. Whether you become a niche blogger or a personal blogger, it can be both great fun and extremely profitable. So what are the keys to running a successful blog? At the heart of it is great content. You want people to come back to your blog again and again and become a regular reader. If you can do that, you will begin to build up a relationship with your readers and they are then more likely to buy your products and services.

Blogs are great for relationship building. They provide the ideal platform to share your knowledge, experience and tips – and allow people to respond back and add in their own comments to the conversation.

I very much hope that you found this guide useful and that it will aid you in setting up your own blog. Blogging isn't rocket science – but it does require thoughtful effort using some of the techniques and ideas we have discussed in this report.

I wish you the very best of luck.